AN ESSAY

ON

THE OXFORD TRACTS.

PRINTED BY NUTTALL AND HODGSON,
GOUGH SQUARE, LONDON.

AN ESSAY

ON

THE OXFORD TRACTS.

BY THE AUTHOR OF
"LETTERS TO THE AUTHORS OF THE PLAIN TRACTS
FOR CRITICAL TIMES."

LONDON:
T. CADELL, STRAND;
AND W. BLACKWOOD AND SONS, EDINBURGH.

M.DCCC.XXXIX.

PREFACE.

In the "Letters to the Authors of the Plain Tracts for Critical times," which he published in January last, the Author of the following Essay advanced and attempted to maintain the following positions: viz.

"That the Church of England is the authority to which we" (those over whom the Church of England is set by the providence of God) "are to resort for the decision of any question which may have arisen, with respect to any point of doctrine or discipline or for the exposition of any passage of Scripture, which admits of diverse and irreconcileable interpretations." And "that" (whilst her authority continues to be recognised), "as against the decision or opinion of the Church of England, as it is propounded in, or to be collected from, her accredited formularies, or is otherwise ascertaintainable, neither private judgment, whether founded upon an interpretation of the English Bible or original Scriptures; nor the opinions of the Fathers, the sanction of tradition, or the testimony of the church universal, is entitled to any authority whatsoever."

" Upon the point adverted to," the Author further stated, " it would be found that he differed most entirely and essentially, not only from the whole of the Low Church party of all denominations; but also, as he feared, from the learned and eminent Authors of the Oxford Tracts."

After the publication of his " Letters to the Authors of the Plain Tracts for Critical Times," the Author directed his attention more particularly to the doctrine taught by the Authors of the Oxford Tracts, with respect to the point adverted to in the preceding extracts, and to various other topics of discussion to which the publication of the Oxford Tracts have given rise; and after a candid inquiry (as he trusts) and mature consideration, he was led to adopt those views upon the subject, which he has attempted to communicate to the reader in the following Essay.

As he has been given to understand that the editorship of the British Critic has been committed to one of the principal authors of the system of the Oxford Tracts, the Author conceives that a few observations in reply to certain remarks upon his " Letters to the Authors of the Plain Tracts," which appeared in the July Number of that Journal, cannot be looked upon as misplaced when inserted in the present publication.

The following extract contains the remarks adverted to :—

"' Letters to the Authors of the Plain Tracts for Critical Times,' are thoughtfully written in defence of baptismal regeneration; and the Author finds ' *upon perusal*, that they directly and most powerfully' tend to ' a breach between the Evangelical and High Church parties,' and, therefore, ' has been led to attempt a refutation of their contents. This is fair. However, with respect to the Oxford Tracts, the Author begs to observe, ' that he has *abstained from the perusal* of them ;' ' yet he has been led to conclude, that ' their system is liable to just exception.' This is not fair?"

Now, the state of the case is simply this: Having incidentally had occasion to allude to the Oxford Tracts, in the passage which has been cited from his Letters to the Authors of the Plain Tracts, and not having read them, for the reason stated in his preface, the Author judged that he was bound to intimate that he had not perused them, in order to render the unfavourable opinion which he had pronounced, conditional only.

The meaning, therefore, which the Author intended to express by the language which he made use of with reference to the Oxford Tracts, in his Preface to the Letters to the Authors of the Plain Tracts, was this :—' that the opinion which he had intimated as to the system of the Authors of the Oxford Tracts being liable to just exception, on account of the doctrine which it inculcated with respect to authority, was founded on a presumption that it inculcated that doctrine (which presumption had arisen from "what he had been able to collect, as to their character and import, from oral disquisitions of which they formed the topic, and from various publications which incidentally refer to them);" and must be admitted to be groundless, and considered as renounced, supposing it proved that the system of the Authors of the Oxford Tracts does not inculcate that doctrine.'

The language made use of with reference to the Oxford Tracts, in the Preface to the Letters to the Authors of the Plain Tracts for Critical Times, is the following :—

" With respect to the Oxford Tracts, to which the Plain Tracts for Critical Times are stated to have " especial reference," the Author begs to observe, that he has abstained from the perusal of them " (from a cause to which it is unnecessary to advert). " But, from what he has been able to collect, as to their character and import, from oral disquisitions of which they have formed the topic, and from various publications which incidentally refer to them, the Author has been led to conclude that the system, as it is the fashion to term it, of the Oxford Tracts, is liable to just exception upon the grounds adverted to in his Ninth Letter," on account, that is, of its inculcating a certain doctrine with respect to authority.

Now we leave it to the intelligent reader to pronounce whether—when he thus unequivocally states 'that he has *not read* the Oxford Tracts, but has been *led to conclude*, from *oral disquisitions* of which they formed the topic, and from *various publications* which incidentally refer to them, that their system is liable to just exception, upon the grounds adverted to, (that is) because they maintain a certain doctrine with respect to 'authority,'—the Author does not fairly and fully express the meaning he intended to convey; and lead an attentive reader to conclude that it is only on the presumption that the *oral disquisitions* and *various publications* adverted to had *rightly* led him to conclude that the Oxford Tracts inculcated the doctrine to which he objects, that he pronounced them " liable to just exception."

Consequently, when the Editor of the British Critic expresses himself as he has done—says, " However, with respect to the Oxford Tracts, the Author begs to observe 'that he has *abstained from the perusal* of them,' yet he has been led to conclude that 'their system is liable to just exception;' this is not fair;"—he does the Author very great injustice.

The commendation, the Author trusts he may

be permitted to observe, which is bestowed upon his former publication, when it is said, in the critical notice referred to, to be " thoughtfully written," outweighs, in the Author's estimation (considering the quarter whence it emanates), whole pages of that indiscriminate and lavish praise which is so much in fashion with reviewers at the present day.

The Author, it will be perceived, has adopted a plan of a somewhat novel character in the structure of his work. It consists, as will be perceived, in his having comprised only that which is essential to the construction of his argument in the text; and thrown all that is not positively essential, however expedient and important its insertion may be, into what he has entitled a 'Justificative Appendix.'

It is possible that the Author's adoption of this plan may be looked upon as an unjustifiable innovation. He was induced (the Author states, lest such should be the case) to adopt the plan in question from having been made practically sensible of the advantages it affords, on the perusal of certain French works, in which a similar arrangement is resorted to, through the medium (so to speak) of the relegation of all unessential matter into what are termed 'Pièces Justificatives.'

Before he concludes these introductory observations, the Author deems it incumbent upon him to state most unreservedly that (according to his judgment) there is much that is truly pious and excellent, as well as just and true, to be found in the numerous capacious volumes in which the Oxford Tracts are now contained.

In conclusion, he ventures to express a hope, that since the Authors of the system of the Oxford Tracts profess, and no doubt sincerely believe themselves, to be influenced by feelings very different from those acrimonious and uncharitable ones which but too often actuate polemical disputants, any discussion which the publication of this Essay may chance to originate, may be conducted in a temperate and amicable spirit, and not with controversial asperity.

CHAPTER I.

THE fundamental error of the authors of the Oxford Tracts consists, as we conceive, in an endeavour to establish a "religious system," which holds the *via media*, as they term it, between the Reformers and the Romanists.

We have only to refer to the Tracts entitled "Via Media,"* in order to ascertain, beyond all possibility of doubt, that it is the design of their authors to establish a religious system which holds the *via media* between the Reformers and the Romanists; or, in other words, between Protestantism as defined to be "the religion of so called freedom and independence, as hating superstition, suspicious of forms, jealous of priestcraft, advocating heart-worship," and Popery.†

Now the truth is, that the *via media* taken by the Church of England, does not lie between the Protestantism spoken of by the writers of the Oxford Tracts and Popery; but between the extreme, and as it were cardinal, errors of Popery and Socinianism.

Between the true *via media* in which the Church

---

* Vide Nos. 38 and 41.   † Vide Justificative Appendix.

of England conducts her obedient disciples, and the extreme error of Socinianism, there lies a wide tract, if we may so speak, within which are divers ways, some of which border upon Socinianism, whilst others diverge but little from the via media taken by our Church: and amongst these is to be found the way holden by that Protestantism spoken of by the authors of the Oxford Tracts.*

Now it is perfectly self-evident that two religious systems—one of which is constituted, so to speak, upon the principle of holding the via media (of preserving the mean, that is, as nearly as possible) between the Reformers—between that Protestantism spoken of by the writers of the Oxford Tracts, and Popery; and the other upon that of holding the via media, of preserving the mean as nearly as possible, between Popery and Socinianism—must necessarily differ on every point upon which Socinianism and the Protestantism spoken of are not of accord.

And since, as we have seen, the system of the authors of the Oxford Tracts is constituted on the former of the principles adverted to; and the orthodox system of the Church of England (for the sake of distinction we are compelled to have recourse to this form of expression) is constituted on the latter; it follows that they will be found to differ upon every point upon which Socinianism and the Protestantism spoken of are not of accord.†

---

* Vide Appendix No. 2. † Vide Appendix No. 3.

That the two systems in question do so differ, is what we propose to point out in the course of the following disquisition.

JUSTIFICATIVE APPENDIX TO CHAP. I.

No. 1.

Upon a perusal of the Tracts entitled "Via Media," it will appear that their authors are under an impression, and assume that the Church of England has taken the via media upon the holding of which the system that they are endeavouring to establish is constituted.

For in No. 38, p. 6, "The glory," they say, "of the Church of England is, that it has taken the *via media*, as it has been called. It lies between the (so called) Reformers and the Romanists." And in No. 41, p. 6, they express themselves to the same effect. "A number of distinct doctrines," they there assert, "are included in the notion of Protestantism, and as to all these, our church has taken the via media between it and Popery."

From their having taken up this impression, the authors of the Oxford Tracts have persuaded themselves, and would leave their readers to infer, that their system is perfectly accordant to, or rather identical with, that of the Church of England. And the consequence is, that whilst they conceive that they are merely engaged in an attempt to promote " a reformation" which shall have the effect of restoring the system of the Church of England to a state from which it has practically degenerated, they are really endeavouring to introduce a system of their own devising which manifestly diverges towards Popery.

No. 2.

It may be observed, that amongst the various ways situate within the tract said to lie between the extreme error of Socinianism and the via media taken by our Church, is to be found that holden by the English orthodox Dissenters, as they are termed; and also that followed by the evangelical party in our Church.

No. 3.

It is of importance to remark, that upon every point upon which there is no variance betwixt the errors holden by Socinianism and the Protestantism spoken of by the authors of the Oxford Tracts, the orthodox system of the Church of England (which is constituted upon the principle of holding the via media between Popery and the former), and the system of the authors of the Oxford Tracts (which is constituted upon the principle of holding the via media between Popery and the latter), may be expected, and will be found, to agree.

The viæ mediæ taken by the two systems, in the case supposed, will run parallel as it were to each other—or rather, will become one and the same. And both, it is obvious, will be at exactly the same distance from the error holden by the Romanists.

For example: Socinianism and the Protestantism spoken of agree in repudiating the doctrine that there is any especial Divine efficacy inherent in the sacraments of Baptism and the Lord's Supper. Consequently, upon this point we may expect, and upon inquiry we shall find, that the system of the authors of the Oxford Tracts and the orthodox system of the Church of England are closely of accord.

Upon referring to the Oxford Tracts, it will appear, that the doctrine asserted by their authors, upon the important points referred to, however startling it may be to the evangelical Churchman, or obnoxious to the Dissenter, is (in the main) strictly accordant to, nay, identical with, that inculcated by the Church of England. The via media therefore taken by the system of the authors of the Oxford Tracts, and that taken by the orthodox system of the Church of England, will, in the case referred to, be one and the same: and the two systems will in consequence be at one and the same distance from the error holden by the Romanists. And this being the case, it is evident that both systems may be expected to be equally inimical to that doctrine in which the cardinal error of Popery, in the case under consideration, principally consists; viz., that of transubstantiation.

It is of the highest importance to remark this, because from the circumstance of the authors of the Oxford Tracts having inveighed against the Popish error of transubstantiation, in language as strong as that in which it has been denounced by the Church of England, the inconsiderate are led to infer that it is impossible that their system can be favourable to Popery; whereas, as will be evident from what we have remarked above, with respect to the Popish doctrine of transubstantiation, the false principle in which, as we conceive, the fundamental error of the system of the authors of the Oxford Tracts consists, is not in operation.

It is from this circumstance, it may be advisable to remark—viz., because the false principle which constitutes the fundamental error of the system of the authors of the Oxford Tracts, is not in operation, with respect to points upon which Socinianism and the Protestantism spoken of are of accord—that much of the danger arising from a propagation of the system is attributable. For, the doctrine taught by the system of the authors of the Oxford Tracts being right (as we conceive) upon the points adverted to, and identical with that inculcated by the Church of England; and it being propounded (as it certainly is) in a manner which displays much learning and sagacity, and with a spirit of candour and good feeling, greatly calculated to facilitate its reception by ingenuous minds, a perusal of the publications in which it is maintained is often attended with the effect which, under such circumstances, we might reasonably look for; viz., that of producing a degree of conviction which leads to its adoption by those by whom it had previously been most strongly reprobated. And such a conviction would naturally—nay, must necessarily—exert an influence (so to speak) which extends far beyond the particular point to which it more immediately relates.

For example: supposing that a person of ingenuous mind, who had previously regarded the doctrine of baptismal regeneration as a poisonous error, were to peruse the Oxford Tracts, and find, as he assuredly would do, that they manifestly prove that that doctrine is taught by the Church of England, and has been ever holden by the Catholic Church, he would be placed in a situation which (as Mr. Newman has most happily remarked, with reference to a different subject) is analogous to that of one who is convinced of the truth of the Copernican system of the universe, after he had long accorded implicit credence to the popular errors it superseded.

Now, one effect of the sudden and entire revolution which has been thus produced in the opinion of the individual of whom we speak, would inevitably be that of occasioning a distrust of that judgment which had led him to adopt the erroneous notion which he entertained and had holden, it may be, from early youth to manhood or old age; and a supreme estimation and respect for the sagacity of those by whom he had been convinced of its unsoundness. And the consequence most assuredly would be, that the individual who had been thus led to distrust his own judgment, and entertain a supreme estimation of the sagacity of the authors of the Oxford Tracts, would resign himself entirely to their guidance, and unreservedly adopt their opinion upon other points. And this being the case, he would unconsciously be led into error with respect to those points upon which there is a variance betwixt the errors holden by Socinianism and the Protestantism spoken of, and when, in consequence, the false principle which constitutes the fundamental error of the system of the authors of the Oxford Tracts is in operation.

CHAPTER II.

ONE very important point upon which a variance is observable betwixt the errors holden by Socinianism and the Protestantism spoken of by the authors of the Oxford Tracts, is that of authority. For the former asserts the supremacy of human reason, and holds that it is not under the necessity of deferring, and should not be constrained to submit itself, to any authority whatsoever; whilst the latter recognises an authority in the Holy Scriptures, to which it holds reason to be subject.

The error holden by the Romanists, with respect to the point of which we speak, consists, as we all know, in the assertion of the doctrine, that an infallible authority has been committed to their Church.

Now the plan which we propose to adopt in order to make good our position, that the system of the authors of the Oxford Tracts does actually and practically differ from the orthodox system of the Church of England, upon points on which Socinianism and the Protestantism spoken of are not of accord, is that of proceeding to inquire,

CHAPTER II.

First, What is the course which, taking the via media between the Socinian error adverted to and that maintained by the Romanists, the orthodox system of the Church of England holds with respect to authority?

Secondly, What is the course which, taking the via media between the error taught by Protestantism spoken of and that maintained by the Romanists, the system of the authors of the Oxford Tracts holds with respect to authority; and

Thirdly, How, and to what extent, the courses repectively holden by the two systems, differ?

But before we enter upon these inquiries, it is essential to ascertain with all possible precision, what is meant by the expression "authority," as it is employed above. By "authority," then, we mean that supreme and uncontrolled, or paramount power of adjudication with respect to doubtful or disputed points, of which it is in the nature of things impossible that two can co-exist. Having premised this, we will proceed to apply ourselves to the first inquiry.

Taking the via media, then, and preserving a mean as nearly as possible between the Socinian error, which asserts the supremacy of human reason, and denies the necessity of its submission to any authority whatsoever, and the Popish error, which ascribes an infallible authority to the Roman Catholic Church, the Church of England assumes authority to herself, but disclaims all pretension to infallibility in the exercise of that authority.

CHAPTER II.

That our Church assumes authority to herself, or (as it may perhaps be expressed with more propriety) asserts that the authority of which we speak has been committed to her, is evident from her XXth Article.

"The Church," she there expressly declares, "hath power to decree rites and ceremonies, and authority in controversies of faith."

Now, inasmuch as it is provided, that "no[*] man shall either print, or preach, to draw the Article aside any way, but shall submit to it in the plain and full meaning thereof: and shall not put his own sense or comment to be the meaning of the Article, but shall take it in the literal and grammatical sense;" and since it is indisputably certain, that when thus taken, the passage cited from the XXth Article must be understood to refer to the Church of England; it is undeniable that our Church has assumed to herself the authority of which we speak—a supreme and uncontrouled or paramount power of adjudication, with respect to doubtful or disputed points.

But in her XXth Article the Church of England also declares, "that it is not lawful for the Church to ordain any thing that is contrary to God's word written; and that beside the same (Holy Writ, that is), it ought not to enforce any thing to be believed for necessity of salvation." Now when she makes this declaration, our Church evidently contemplates the possibility

---

[*] Vide the Declaration prefixed to the Articles.

of her ordaining what may be contrary to God's word, or attempting to enforce something not contained in Holy Writ to be believed for necessity of salvation; and, consequently, by making it, she virtually confesses herself liable to err, and must be holden to disclaim all pretension to infallibility in the exercise of the authority which we have seen that she assumes.*

And now, having ascertained what is the course which, taking the via media between the error taught by Socinianism and that maintained by the Romanists, the orthodox system of the Church of England holds with respect to authority, and found that it consists in her assuming an authority to herself, and at the same time disclaiming all pretension to infallibility in the exercise of that authority; let us proceed to inquire,

In the second place, What is the course which, taking the via media between the error taught by the Protestantism spoken of † and that maintained by the Romanists, the system of the authors of the Oxford Tracts holds with respect to authority.

Upon prosecuting this inquiry, we find that, according to the system of the authors of the Oxford

---

* Vide Justificative Appendix to Chapter II.

† It consists in a belief, that the authority spoken of resides in the Holy Scriptures—in certain writings, that is, which are arbitrarily assumed to constitute the Holy Scriptures—as interpreted by private judgment.

Tracts, the authority of which we speak is holden to reside in Catholic or primitive tradition.

That such is the case will be evident, when we refer, as we propose to do, to the well known sermon on Primitive Tradition, delivered, and subsequently published, by an eminent divine, who is understood to be one of the contributors to the Oxford Tracts.

In the sermon in question, after contending (whether successfully or not, we do not pretend to decide) that the " trust or deposit," which St. Paul exhorts Timothy to keep, " was the treasure of apostolical doctrines and church rules; the rules and doctrines which make up the charter of Christ's kingdom;" " Must it not be owned," Mr. Keble asks, " that Timothy's deposit did comprise matter independent of and distinct from the truths which are directly Scriptural?" " The truths and rules committed to Timothy's charge were at the time almost or wholly unwritten*," Mr. Keble asserts in the next paragraph; and in the succeeding one he adds, in corroboration of his statement,

" As often as Tertullian and Irenæus have false preachers to reprove, or unevangelical corruptions to expose, do they not refer to the tradition of the whole church, as to something independent of the written word, and sufficient at that time to refute heresy even alone?"

---

* Vide p. 21.

"It may help," Mr. Keble continues, "to the understanding and application of the whole argument, if I point out three distinct fields of Christian knowledge, in neither of which can we advance satisfactorily, or safely, without constant appeal to tradition, such as has been described."*

The first is *the system and arrangement of fundamental articles.* The second great subject is *the interpretation of Scripture.* "Catholic tradition bears upon Scripture interpretation," Mr. Keble observes in explanation, "not only indirectly, by supplying, as just now stated, certain great landmarks of apostolical doctrine, conformably to which the written statements are all to be interpreted; but also in numerous cases directly; setting the Church's seal" (or, in other words, adjudicating authoritatively) "upon one among many possible expositions of particular passages."

That Mr. Keble ascribes the authority of which we speak to primitive or Catholic tradition, is rendered indubitably clear by the above passages cited from his sermon.† And that the same doctrine is asserted in the Tracts, will be evident from the folfollowing extract.

In the Tract (No. 78), which is entitled "Catena Patrum," and contains a statement of the opinions of certain eminent divines, adduced by the authors of

---

* Page 34. † Vide Appendix, No. II.

the Oxford Tracts, with a view of confirming and illustrating the doctrine which they hold with respect to tradition, we find the following passage: "If a doctrine is propounded to me, as virtually essential, that is, to speak technically, as matter of faith, before I receive it as such, I must go to the Catholic succession, and ascertain whether that doctrine has been held *semper, ubique, ab omnibus.*"*

Now, from the above cited passage, it is incontestably evident that Bishop Jebb (whose opinion it expresses) conceives, and that the authors of the Oxford Tracts, who have adduced it in corroboration of their views upon the subject, must be understood to maintain, that the authority of which we speak resides in what the Bishop terms the Catholic succession, or, in other words, in Catholic or primitive tradition.

It now only remains to inquire, in the third place, how, and to what extent, the courses which we have shewn to be those respectively taken by the two systems, differ?

It is self-evident that they are absolutely contrariant.

For if I believe and acknowledge that the authority of which we speak resides in the Church of England (as we have seen that it does, according to the orthodox system of our church), if any doctrine

---

* Vide Appendix, No. III.

is propounded to me, I must go to the Church of England and ascertain what (if any) is the decision or opinion which she pronounces upon the point; and when I have ascertained the decision or opinion, pronounced by the Church of England, I shall implicitly defer to it, and be content, if need be, to whistle primitive tradition down the wind—to hold, that is, any contrary decision or opinion, established by a reference to primitive tradition, as wholly unauthoritative and nugatory.

But if, on the contrary, I believe and acknowledge that the authority of which we speak, resides in Catholic or primitive tradition; then, when a doctrine is propounded to me, I must go to the Catholic succession, or primitive tradition, and ascertain what is the decision or arbitrament which it pronounces; and having ascertained this, I shall accept such arbitrament; and regarding it as decisive of the matter in doubt, I shall attach no importance to any contrary opinion or decision which the Church of England may pronounce.

JUSTIFICATIVE APPENDIX TO CHAP. II.

It will possibly be urged, that, according to the view of the subject exhibited above, it is evident that the authority which the Church of England has assumed must be nominal only; because by disclaiming all pretension to infallibility, and thereby, as a necessary consequence, leaving every man at liberty to question whether any decision or opinion which she pronounces in the exercise of that authority be right or wrong, she subjects the authority which she has ostensibly assumed, to the private judgment of every individual. But this is not the case.

For since, as we have seen, the Church of England has assumed authority to herself, it follows, as a necessary consequence, that every member of her communion is bound to recognise and defer to that authority. And no man can openly and advisedly question whether any decision or opinion, pronounced by the Church of England in the exercise of the authority which she has assumed, be not wrong, without having virtually disclaimed that authority; for had he continued to recognise it, in deference to it, he must necessarily have admitted that the Church was right.

The case stands simply thus. A man must either recognise the authority which we have seen that the Church of England has assumed—in which case he will have recourse to, and accept her adjudication upon doubtful or disputed points; or not recognize it—in which case he will reject the adjudication of the Church of England upon doubtful or disputed points, and must of necessity refer them to some other arbitrament. But a man cannot defer to the authority of the Church of England, and accept her adjudication upon one point, and disclaim her authority, and reject her arbitrament upon another, according to his will and pleasure. Consequently it is evident, that by disclaiming all pretension to infallibility, in the exercise of the authority which she has assumed, the Church of England does not subject that authority to the private judgment of every individual. By doing so, she leaves men at liberty to question whether any decision or opinion which she may pronounce, be right—or, in other words, at liberty to disclaim her authority; but not at liberty to reject her adjudication upon doubtful or disputed points, whilst they continue to recognise her authority.

But it will doubtless be contended, that if the case be thus; if (as has been stated) by disclaiming all pretension to infallibility in the exercise of the authority which she has assumed, our Church leaves a man at liberty to question whether any decision or opinion which she pronounces in the exercise of that authority be not wrong—which he cannot do without disclaming her authority, and, if he act consistently, renouncing communion with her; it will follow, that dissent must be not only well nigh universal, but at the same time perfectly justifiable; it must be granted that our Church may be said to leave a man at liberty to secede from her communion whenever he questions whether any decision or opinion which she has pronounced be right.

Now if the relation between the Church of England and her members were as simple as it appears to be according to the statement given above, the position for which we have supposed an objector to contend, must be admitted to be tenable: but the relation which subsists between the Church of England and her members is not thus simple; it is complicated (so to speak) and greatly modified by the circumstance that there is another party—we beg that we may not be supposed to speak irreverently, when we express ourselves thus plainly, for the sake of precision—interested in its maintenance, viz., the Lord God Almighty.

God has commanded all men to submit themselves to those who have the spiritual rule over them, who are set over them in the Lord.

This command, it is clear, enjoins submission to the constituted form of spiritual authority set over any man, or any body of men, by the providence of God.

Now the constituted form of spiritual authority set over every native of this land by the providence of God, is the National Church—the Church of England.

Consequently every member of our Church* is commanded, by a Divine injunction, to submit himself to her authority.

---

* It is self-evident that the above and the following observations will apply with equal force to the case of every native of the land. And should these pages chance to fall into the hands of any conscientious and ingenuous Dissenter, the author trusts that the doubt which they must have the effect of suggesting, as to the soundness of his creed, will be instrumental in inducing such an one to a careful re-examination of what he regards as the 'grounds which legitimate his secession. He has expressly confined his observations

Now this being the case, it is certain, beyond all possibility of doubt, that although, from the circumstance of her having disclaimed all pretension to infallibility in the exercise of the authority which she has assumed, our Church necessarily leaves men at liberty to question whether any decision or opinion which she has pronounced in the exercise of that authority, be not wrong; although they cannot do so advisedly, without disclaiming her authority, and thereby virtually renouncing communion with her; yet, being commanded by God to submit themselves to those who have the spiritual rule over them—to that constituted form of spiritual authority set over them by the providence of God; and the constituted form of spiritual authority set over every member of our Church being the Church of England, every member of our Church is bound to defer to the authority of the Church of England with respect to every point which is not of fundamental moment. If men refuse to do this, where is their submission to those who have the spiritual rule over them?—where is their obedience to the Divine command by which such submission is enjoined?

But, inasmuch as it is evident that the Divine injunction, by which men are commanded to submit themselves to those who are set over them in the Lord, must be understood as limited by the necessary exception that they do not enjoin any thing of fundamental moment which is essentially wrong; it follows that, notwithstanding that Divine injunction, it cannot be unlawful for any man to entertain a doubt whether the constituted form of spiritual authority under which he has been placed by the providence of God, do not enjoin some doctrine or other matter of fundamental moment which is essentially wrong; nor can it be unallowable for one who has been led to entertain any such doubt, to question advisedly whether the case be so, although he cannot do this without disclaiming the authority of those who have the spiritual rule over him.

Now the case being thus, it becomes evident, that although, with respect to every point which is not of fundamental mo-

---

(the author begs to state) to the case of professed members of the Church of England, in order to avoid involving himself in controversy with her inveterate enemies.

ment, the members of our Church are constrained to defer implicitly to her authority, in obedience to the Divine injunction which commands men to submit themselves to those who have the spiritual rule over them; yet, with respect to any point which is of fundamental moment, it cannot be unlawful for any member of the Church of England to doubt whether she do not enjoin some doctrine or other matter of fundamental moment which is essentially wrong, nor unallowable for him to question advisedly whether the case be so, although he cannot do this without disclaiming her authority.

We see, therefore, that whatever might have been the case, had the relation between the Church of England and her members been simple (which it is not), since (as the case is) it is complicated or modified in the manner we have pointed out, the members of our Church are constrained to submit themselves to her authority with respect to every point which is not of fundamental moment: but that, with respect to points which are of fundamental moment, because the Divine injunction by which men are commanded to submit themselves to those who have the spiritual rule over them must be understood as limited by the necessary exception that they do not enjoin any thing of fundamental moment which is essentially wrong, and inasmuch as the Church of England has disclaimed all pretension to infallibility, in the exercise of the authority which she has assumed, it is allowable for any member of our Church who may be led to entertain a doubt whether any decision or opinion which she may have pronounced with respect to any point of fundamental moment, be not essentially wrong, to question advisedly whether the case be so, although he cannot do this without disclaiming her authority.

But here a most important question suggests itself. How is one who thus advisedly questions whether any decision or opinion pronounced by the Church of England with respect to a point of fundamental moment, be not essentially wrong, to satisfy himself that such is or is not the case?—or, to state the case generally, to what authority must the man who has disclaimed the authority of the Church of England, appeal for an arbitrament upon any doubtful or disputed point?

'That he must have recourse to the Scriptures'—to the authorised English version of the Bible, that is; 'that the authority to which such an one should appeal is the Bible,'—the English Bible; is the commonly received opinion.

The fallaciousness of this opinion is self-evident. For when a man disclaims the authority of the Church of England, it stands to reason that he must at the same time renounce all confidence in the authorized English version of the Bible—in that canon or compilation, reading, and translation of the Scriptures, which derives its sanction from the authority he has disclaimed.

But it being granted (as it must be) that the individual of whom we speak cannot have recourse to the English Bible, the question recurs, 'Whither must he resort?'—'to what authority must he appeal?'

We answer 'To a canon or compilation and reading of the Holy Scriptures framed by the exercise of his private judgment—framed by the exercise of that same private judgment which has led him to disclaim the authority of the Church of England.'

Or, to express ourselves more particularly. One who has the misfortune (for such it most undoubtedly would be to an ingenuous mind) to find himself called upon to disclaim the authority of the Church of England, must, out of the many and varying writings which purport to be, or are supposed or asserted to constitute, the Holy Scriptures, or inspired writings which contain a revelation of the will of God, frame a canon or compilation and reading which he can confidently rely upon as containing the Holy Scriptures, or inspired writings which contain a revelation of the will of God, by the exercise of his private judgment. And to this canon or compilation and reading of the Holy Scriptures, framed by the exercise of his private judgment, he must resort or appeal, in order to determine whether the Church of England do or do not enjoin any doctrine of fundamental moment which is essentially wrong, or for an arbitrament upon any other matter in doubt.

But this being admitted, another equally momentous question presents itself—'When (as he must do) he attempts to frame a canon or compilation and reading of the Holy Scriptures, which he can confidently rely upon as comprising the inspired writings which contain a revelation of the will of God, by the exercise of his private judgment, how is the individual of whom we speak to proceed?' It is indisputably certain, that it must be by a responsible and reasonable, and not by an unrestricted and licentious, exercise of his private judgment, that the individual of whom we speak must proceed in his attempt to frame a canon or compilation and reading of the Holy Scriptures. It must be by an exercise of his private judgment, not regulated by his will and pleasure, whim or humour, but conducted according to right reason and conformably to the dictates of an enlightened conscience.

Now, this being granted, (and it is undeniable)—and inasmuch as the legal rule of evidence, which prescribes 'that in every case the best evidence of which the nature of the case will admit, must be resorted to,' is strictly accordant to right reason; it follows that one who is engaged in framing a canon or compilation and reading of the Holy Scriptures, by the exercise of his private judgment, must have respect to it.

Now, when engaged in framing a canon or compilation and reading out of the many and varying writings which purport to be, and are supposed or asserted to contain, the inspired writings which contain a revelation of the will of God, the individual of whom we speak will assuredly meet with variations which he cannot reconcile, and find himself involved in doubt with respect to the authenticity of particular passages, and the canonical character (so to speak) of particular books. Now, upon referring to the writings of the early Christian writers, or fathers of the church, he will find that their contents often decide in favour of one and against another of the variations alluded to; or authenticate one passage and discredit another passage of the manuscripts consulted. And, inasmuch as the writings of the early Christian writers, some of which are cotemporaneous with the manuscripts consulted, constitute the best evidence of which the nature of the case will admit; and since, as we have seen, the individual of whom we speak is bound to have respect to that legal rule of evidence which prescribes ' that the best evidence of which the nature of the case will admit, must be resorted to,' it is clear that in the instance of which we speak he is bound to receive, and will be under the necessity of deferring to, the opinions of the Fathers.

Again: in the various manuscripts which he has occasion to consult, the individual who is engaged in framing a canon or compilation and reading of the Holy Scriptures by the exercise of his private judgment, will meet with statements which he is unable to reconcile to his satisfaction. Now one of these statements may possibly be consistent with, and the other opposed to, the universal practice of the primitive church, as handed down to us by tradition; and in that case, tradition will constitute the best evidence of which the nature of the case will admit, against the one and in favour of the other of these irreconcileable statements. And that being the case, the individual of whom we speak will be bound to have respect to, and abide by, what it testifies.

And since the individual who is engaged in framing a canon or compilation and reading of the Holy Scripture by an exercise of his private judgment accordant to right reason, is compellable (under certain circumstances) to decide acccording to the opinions of the Fathers, and to abide by what tradition declares, it follows that he must (under certain circumstances) of necessity defer to, and virtually acknowledge an authority to reside in, the Fathers and tradition.

The sum of what has been said in the course of the above lengthened, but (as we trust) not needlessly prolix, observations, is this.

So long as the authority of the Church of England is recognised, the decision or opinion of the Church of England, as it is pronounced in her accredited documents and formularies, or may hereafter be declared by any " sacred synod of the nation, in the name of Christ, and by the king's authority assembled,"* must be primarily resorted to for an arbitrament upon any doubtful or disputed point. And supposing it appear that the Church of England has not directly pronounced any

---

* Vide 139th Canon.

decision or opinion upon the matter in question, the authorised English version of the Bible should be resorted to in the second place; inasmuch as it contains that canon or compilation and reading of the writings which purport to be, and are supposed or asserted to contain, the Holy Scriptures, which the Church of England has sanctioned and authenticates. And in either case—viz., as against the arbitrament pronounced upon a resort to the decision or opinion of the Church of England, or as against one which may be obtained upon a reference to the authorised English version of the Bible—the opinions of the Fathers and the testimony of tradition will not be entitled to any authority whatsoever, cannot be resorted to or received.

But the moment that the authority of the Church of England is disclaimed, the case becomes altogether different. Then the decision or opinion of the Church of England, either pronounced directly in the manner we have mentioned, or through the medium (so to speak) of the authorized English version of the Bible, will not be entitled to any weight whatsoever—cannot be resorted to, or received: whilst, in that case, the opinions of the Fathers and the testimony of tradition will (under certain circumstances) be entitled to authority, and must necessarily be received and deferred to.

The following practical instance may, possibly, serve to place what we have said in a clearer point of view.

Let us suppose that A. B. and C. D., two members of the Church of England, who (as such) recognise the authority which we have seen that she assumes, differ in opinion with respect to regeneration; the one holding that regeneration is wrought by virtue of a Divine efficacy inherent in the sacrament of Baptism—or is baptismal, in other words; and the other maintaining that it is effected by the independent agency of the Holy Ghost, and is not baptismal.

Now, as A. B. and C. D. agree in recognising the authority of the Church of England, they will of course refer the decision of the question in dispute to her arbitrament. Upon doing so, they will find that our Church pronounces an adjudication in favour of the opinion holden by A. B. as distinctly and decisively as it is possible for her to do—as it is possible for an arbitrament to be.

Let us suppose, moreover, that in common with many professed members of our Church, C.D. conceives that the doctrine of baptismal regeneration is a poisonous error, and also accounts it (as it certainly is) one of fundamental moment. Now, this being the case, when apprized of the distinct and decisive arbitrament which the Church of England pronounces in favour of baptismal regeneration, C.D. will assuredly be led to question, advisedly, 'whether when she teaches that men are made regenerate, and become members of Christ, children of God, and inheritors of the kingdom of heaven, at their baptism, our Church does not inculcate a doctrine of fundamental moment which is essentially wrong?' And he cannot do this (as we have seen) without disclaiming the authority of the Church of England. And having disclaimed the authority of the Church of England, he cannot (as we have seen) resort or appeal to the English version of the Bible; but must frame a canon or compilation and reading of the Scriptures by an exercise of his private judgment, conducted according to right reason and conformably to the dictates of an enlightened conscience; and in doing this, he will (in certain circumstances) be under the necessity of deferring to, and recognising an authority in, the Fathers and tradition. And having succeeded in framing a canon or compilation of the Scriptures which he can confidently rely upon as comprising the inspired writings which contain a revelation of the will of God, by the exercise of his private judgment, C. D. must resort to that canon or compilation and reading of the Scriptures, in order to determine whether the Church of England does or does not inculcate a doctrine of fundamental moment which is essentially wrong, when she teaches that men are made regenerate at baptism.

It may be observed, moreover, that when C.D. has succeeded in framing a canon or compilation and reading of the Scriptures which he can confidently rely upon as comprising the inspired writings which contain a revelation of the will of God, and proceeds to appeal to it, in order to determine whether the doctrine of baptismal regeneration, as taught by the Church of England, is or is not essentially wrong, he may chance to find himself involved in difficulty with respect to the interpretation of particular passages of the canon or compilation and reading of the Scriptures which he has framed; and being under the necessity of proceeding in his attempt to elucidate any such difficulty by an exercise of his private judgment which is accordant to right reason (as will be the case), C. D. will be constrained to adopt the exposition given by the Fathers, or that authenticated by tradition, as often as a resort to the one or the other, chances to supply the most satisfactory elucidation of the difficulty which perplexes him: and thus he will again be under the necessity of deferring to, and recognising an authority in, the Fathers and tradition.

We have but one more remark to add to these lengthened observations. It is this:

That when we have stated, in the course of them, that one who has disclaimed the authority of the Church of England, will, under certain circumstances, be under the necessity of deferring to, and recognising an authority in, the Fathers and tradition, we do not conceive, we would not be understood to assert, that the authority of the Fathers and tradition is paramount over that of Scripture. The authority possessed by the Fathers and tradition in the instance adverted to is adventitious, as it were, (we conceive), and of a temporary character—is but an authority *in transitu*, if we may so speak.

The case we conceive stands thus: If it be granted (as it universally is by all who profess the Christian religion) that certain inspired writings are extant, which contain a revelation of the will of God, it stands to reason that those inspired writings must constitute the paramount jurisdiction (if we may so speak) to which one who has disclaimed the specific spiritual authority to which he has providentially been subjected, must appeal for an arbitrament upon any doubtful or disputed point. And although, when, he attempts (as he must do) to frame a canon or compilation and reading of the Scriptures, upon which he can confidently rely as containing a revelation of the will of God, by an exercise of his private judgment conducted according to right reason, such an one will be constrained to defer to the opinions of the Fathers, and rely upon the testimony of tradition, and by so doing virtually recognises their authority; yet, the authority which he so recognises, is so far temporary only and adventitious, that the passage or book, as the case may be, which it authenticates, when so authenticated, and regarded, in consequence, as a part of the inspired writings which contain a revelation of the will of God, must of necessity become entitled to, and be invested with, that paramount jurisdiction of which we speak; except on one single event, viz., unless the writings of the Fathers, and those in which the testimony of tradition has been handed down to us, can be shewn to be of equal inspiration with the Holy Scriptures, or inspired writings containing a revelation of the will of God, which are universally admitted to be extant.

For example: supposing, for the sake of argument, that an individual who has disclaimed the specific spiritual authority under which he has been placed, and proceeds in consequence to frame a canon of Scripture by the exercise of his private judgment, were to admit St. Paul's Epistle to the Hebrews into such canon, in deference to the opinions of the Fathers, or from a regard to the testimony of tradition. In that case, if a doctrine established by any passage in St. Paul's Epistle to the Hebrews, were found to be irreconcileable with the opinions of the Fathers, or contrary to the testimony of tradition, the scriptural adjudication (if we may so speak) pronounced by such passage, must be received and deferred to, notwithstanding it opposes itself to those Fathers and to that tradition from which St. Paul's Epistle to the Hebrews had received its authentication as Scripture.

No. 2.

We feel called upon to acknowledge the general excellence of Mr. Keble's discourse, and to admit that (as it appears to us) his arguments are (in themselves) entitled to much weight, and likely to be highly serviceable in the cause of truth; but they are rendered inadmissible, we conceive, in the case under consideration, by the accident (so to speak) of their being addressed to Clergymen of the Church of England, who are (as such) bound to recognise the authority of the Church of England.

For example: When, addressing himself to a congregation of Clergymen of the Church of England, Mr. Keble tells them (as he does amongst many other observations of a similar purport) that "Catholic tradition bears upon Scriptural interpretation, not only indirectly, by supplying certain great landmarks of apostolical doctrine, conformably to which the written statements are all to be interpreted; but also, in numerous cases, directly; setting the Church's seal" (or in other words, adjudicating authoritatively) "upon one among many possible expositions of particular passages," he says that which has a direct tendency to mislead; for if (as we trust we have indisputably shewn) the Church of England has assumed authority to herself, it is to her decision or opinion pronounced in the manner mentioned above, that Clergymen of the Church of England, in common with all who recognise her authority, must look for an authoritative exposition of particular passages of Holy Writ. For instance: supposing one who recognises the authority of the Church of England were to entertain a doubt as to the interpretation of the passage of Scripture which records our Saviour's interview with Nicodemus, or as to the interpretation of any of the many passages in St. Paul's Epistles, in which faith is spoken of; upon ascertaining that (in the former case) in several of her formularies (in her Catechism for instance, and her services for Baptism and Confirmation), and (in the latter case) in certain of her Homilies, the Church of England authoritatively pronounces an exposition of the passages in question, or "sets her seal (as Mr. Keble says) upon one among many possible expositions of them," the individual of whom we speak will unhesitatingly subscribe to that exposition as the true one.

But had Mr. Keble addressed himself to a congregation of Dissenting ministers, or others who avowedly repudiate the authority of the Church of England, what he told them, when he expressed himself to the effect above stated, would have been not only essentially, but also circumstantially true; or, to express ourselves more fully, Mr. Keble's observations, as to the authority to which tradition is entitled with respect to the interpretation Scripture, would, in the case supposed, have been not only true in themselves, but also at the same time strictly applicable, and conducive to the establishment of a just conclusion.

No. 3.

We have been led to refer more particularly to the opinion of the late Bishop Jebb, not only because it is one of the very few out of the numerous collection of opinions of which the Catena Patrum consists, which is really in point; but also because (as we conceive) the late Bishop Jebb, and his friend and correspondent Alexander Knox, may be regarded as the originators of the system of the authors of the Oxford Tracts. For there are few (if any) of the positions or opinions advanced by the authors of the Oxford Tracts, in the course of their voluminous publications, of which the germ is not discoverable in the Correspondence or other productions of Knox and Jebb.

That by far, the great majority of the opinions of which the several catenæ Patrum adduced by the authors of the Oxford Tracts consists, are not in point—do not, that is, in any degree affect the state of the question, ' whether the doctrine taught by the orthodox system of the Church of England, with respect to authority, or that holden by the system of the authors of the Oxford Tracts' be right—will be immediately evident, upon a reference to them.

Bishop Jewell, for instance, (we take the first opinion adduced) is directing what he says, when he appeals to " the authority of the Scriptures and of the old doctors and councils," against "our adversaries,"—against the open enemies of the Church of England, that is. Consequently it is in a case in which the authority of the Church of England has been disclaimed, that he so appeals to the authority of the Scriptures, and of the old doctors and councils. It is evident, therefore, that the opinion expressed by Bishop Jewell in the instance which has been adduced by the authors of the Oxford Tracts, in confirmation of the doctrine which they maintain with respect to authority, does not support that doctrine as against, or to the prejudice of, the doctrine which we have shewn to be that holden by the orthodox system of the Church of England.

CHAPTER II.

In order to shew that the opinion expressed by Bishop Jewell supports the doctrine taught by the system of the authors of the Oxford Tracts, as against that holden by the orthodox system of the Church of England, a case should have been adduced in which Bishop Jewell (like Bishop Jebb and Mr. Keble) directs members of our Church to go (as Bishop Jebb expresses it) to " the old doctors and councils," for an adjudication upon a point on which the Church of England has authoritatively pronounced a decision.

It is needless to proceed with our examination of the Catenæ Patrum. For it is indisputably certain, that on a careful perusal, or upon a reference (where necessary) to the works from which they have been extracted, every opinion they contain will be found to be propounded either in a case in which the authority of the Church of England has been, or is assumed to be disclaimed, or in one in which it has not been, or cannot be assumed to be disclaimed. In the former case, the opinion cited will not conduce in any degree whatever to the support of the doctrine taught by the system of the Authors of the Oxford Tracts, as against that holden by the orthodox system of the Church of England: and in the latter, if it be true that the Church of England has assumed authority to herself, the opinion cited must be pronounced to be erroneous, (so far as it supports the doctrine taught by the system of the Authors of the Oxford Tracts, as against that holden by the orthodox system of the Church of England,) however high may be the reputation of the individual by whom it is asserted.

CHAPTER III.

ANOTHER important point upon which a variance is observable betwixt the errors holden by Socinianism and the Protestantism spoken of by the authors of the Oxford Tracts, is with respect to the character or qualification conferred upon the ministers of religion on their appointment.

For denying that there is any Holy Ghost, Socinianism must necessarily hold that its ministers do not receive any description of assistance from Him in the discharge of the duties of their office. Whereas, believing that the assistance of the Holy Ghost is necessary to the efficacious discharge of the duties of a minister of religion, the Protestantism spoken of maintains that such assistance is vouchsafed.

The tenet that such assistance is vouchsafed to individuals, by whomsoever appointed, in answer to the prayers of those who assist at their appointment; or in other words, by virtue of an influence extrinsic of, and wholly unconnected with, the apostolic rite of ordination, is that which constitutes the error of the Protestantism spoken of, with respect to the point we are considering.

CHAPTER III.

The error holden by the Romanists upon the point, may be stated to consist in their maintaining that Holy Orders is a sacrament—is a sacrament, that is, in the recognised and legitimate sense of the word; viz., an outward and visible sign, whereby an inward and spiritual grace is conferred upon the individual ordained.*

In proceeding to consider the subject to which our attention has been called, we propose to resort to the same method of treating it, as that which we adopted with respect to the last question discussed—viz., to inquire,

First, What is the course which, taking the via media between the Socinian error adverted to and that holden by the Romanists, the orthodox system of the Church of England holds with respect to ordination?

Secondly, What is the course which, professing, and no doubt intending, to take the via media between the error maintained by the Protestantism spoken of, and that holden by the Romanists, the system of the authors of the Oxford Tracts holds with respect to ordination?

Thirdly, How, and to what extent, the courses respectively taken by the two systems differ?

Taking the via media between the Socinian error, which maintains that the ministers of religion do not

---

* Vide Justificative Appendix.

receive any description of assistance from the Holy Ghost, and the Romish error, which holds that Holy Orders is a sacrament, the orthodox system of the Church of England teaches 'that ordination is a sacred commission of Christ's institution, which is attended with an unction from the Holy Ghost, that operates (so to speak) exclusively for the benefit of the Church, and does not confer grace upon the individual.'

That the doctrine taught by the Church of England, with respect to ordination, is such as we have stated above, will become evident (as we trust) upon a due consideration of the following remarks.

Our Church most distinctly, and we may add, most authoritatively, holds, that personal grace in the individual is not necessary to the efficacious discharge of the office of a minister of the Gospel.

In her XXVIth Article she declares, that, "Although, in the visible church, the evil be ever mingled with the good, and sometimes the evil have chief authority in the ministration of the word and sacraments; yet forasmuch as they do not the same in their own name, but in Christ's, and do minister by His commission and authority, we may use their ministry, both in hearing the word of God, and receiving of the sacraments. Neither is the effect of Christ's ordinance taken away by their wickedness, nor the grace of God's gifts diminished, from such as by faith, and rightly, do receive the sacraments ministered unto them; which be effectual because of Christ's institution and promise, although they be ministered by evil men."

It is certain, therefore, beyond all possibility of doubt, that, according to the orthodox system of the Church of England, the conferring of any description or degree of personal grace upon the individual ordained, is not necessary to render ordination efficacious for the benefit of the Church. And inasmuch as there is nothing in the Article cited to warrant a conclusion that it is not as applicable to the case of an individual who was wicked at the time of his ordination, as it is to that of one who becomes wicked afterwards, it is equally undeniable that its contents establish the position that, according to the orthodox system of the Church of England, ordination does not necessarily confer grace upon the individual.

Now it will probably be urged, ' that although (as the Church of England has plainly pronounced) the communication of inward and spiritual or personal grace to the individual ordained, is not necessary to render ordination efficacious for the benefit of the Church; yet, inasmuch as the duties of a minister of the Gospel are especially arduous and important, the communication of personal grace to the individual ordained, may be necessary for his own sake :' and ' that such communication of personal grace is necessary, and is so holden to be by our church, and may be, and is, conferred in some cases at ordination, though not in all,' may perhaps be contended.

But be it observed, that such is the estimation in which our Church holds " The high mystery (as she terms it) of the sacrament of the Lord's Supper,* that it is evident she accounts it as a means of grace adequate to the supply of the spiritual necessities (be they greater or less) of every worthy communicant.

Now this being the case—since our Church accounts the sacrament of the Lord's Supper a means of grace adequate to the supply of the spiritual necessities (be they greater or less) of every worthy communicant; it is evident that, in the judgment of our Church, the communication of any description or degree of personal grace at ordination must be needless.

And that our Church is not inconsistent in this respect, but holds (in conformity with her belief, that the communication of personal grace at ordination is needless) that ordination does not confer personal grace upon the individual ordained, is practically demonstrated by the fact that she has prescribed the administration of the Sacrament of the Lord's Supper as a part of her Ordination Service.†

It is evident, therefore, that, according to the orthodox system of the Church of England, 'ordina-

---

* Vide Homily XVII. † Vide Appendix, No. 2.

tion is a sacred commission of Christ's institution, which is attended with an unction from the Holy Ghost that operates exclusively for the benefit of the Church, and does not confer grace upon the individual.'

Let us now proceed, in the second place, to inquire what is the course taken by the system of the authors of the Oxford Tracts, with respect to ordination.

Taking, or rather professing, and no doubt intending, to take, the via media between the error maintained by the Protestantism spoken of, and that holden by Popery, with respect to ordination, the system of the authors of the Oxford Tracts teaches 'that ordination is a rite which confers a special description and degree of personal grace upon the individual ordained.'

In the Tract (No. 1.), which is entitled "Thoughts on the Ministerial Commission," and consists of, and purports to be, an address from a Presbyter to the Clergy, after citing the words in which the Priesthood is committed by the Church of England; viz. "Receive the Holy Ghost for the office and work of a Priest, in the Church of God, now committed unto thee," &c.; "These," I say, it proceeds, "were words spoken to us, and received by us, when we were brought nearer to God than at any other time of our lives."

Now since the individual ordained is brought *nearer to God*, at ordination, than he was before, or than he could ever have been, had he not been ordained (as is plainly intimated by the extract which we have cited from the Tract No. 1), it is clear beyond all possibility of doubt, that ordination must confer a special description and degree of personal grace.

We may, therefore, safely pronounce that, according to the system of the authors of the Oxford Tracts, 'ordination is a rite which confers a special description and degree of personal grace upon the individual ordained.'*

We proceed, in the third place, to inquire how the course which we have ascertained to be that holden by the orthodox system of the Church of England, and that taken, as we have seen, by the system of the authors of the Oxford Tracts, differs?

We have seen that, according to the orthodox system of the Church of England, 'ordination is a sacred commission of Christ's institution, which is attended with an unction from the Holy Ghost, that operates exclusively for the benefit of the Church, and does not confer grace upon the individual ordained'; and that, according to the system of the authors of the Oxford Tracts, 'ordination is a rite which confers a special description and degree of personal grace upon the individal ordained; con-consequently' it is self-evident that the two systems differ irreconcileably—are directly contrariant upon the point.

---

* Vide Appendix, No. 3.

JUSTIFICATIVE APPENDIX TO CHAP. III.

It may at first sight appear that there is nothing very pernicious or objectionable in this error of the Romanists. But a very slight degree of consideration will enable any one to perceive that it leads to—indeed might be said to involve—several of the most pernicious of the Romish errors.

For it is impossible to hold, that ordination confers any description or degree of inward and personal grace, without at the same time admitting that the ordained individual is raised to a higher spiritual state than the unordained layman can by any possibility attain unto; or is invested, in other words, with a superiority of spiritual being. For both priest and layman being endued in common with the inward and spiritual grace, which the Sacraments of Baptism and the Lord's Supper are appointed to convey; and the priest being endued, over and above the grace received by him in common with the layman, with an inward and spiritual or personal grace conferred at ordination; it follows that, supposing the priest and the layman to be equally diligent in improving the grace given to them, the priest by virtue of the additional grace of ordination, of which he was the exclusive participant, will attain to an elevation of spiritual character to which it is impossible for the layman to reach. And he, therefore, may very reasonably be said to be invested, as we have said, with a superiority of spiritual being.

And when this supposed truth is once admitted—when it is believed that the priest is endued with a superiority of spiritual being, an inordinate and superstitious veneration for the priesthood must be the inevitable consequence. And every one who has the slightest acquaintance with the subject under discussion, must be well aware how many and pernicious are the practical Romish errors which have their source (so to speak) in an inordinate and superstitious veneration for the priesthood.

No. 2.

It will perhaps be contended that there are certain expressions to be found in the formularies of our Church, which appear to intimate that she holds that ordination conveys some description or degree of personal grace.

But before we go the length of concluding that our church is chargeable with inconsistency in this respect, it will behove us to inquire whether it be not possible to reconcile the fact (which for the sake of argument we will admit,) that she uses language which appears to intimate that she deems that ordination conveys some description or degree of personal grace, with the fact, that she holds that ordination operates exclusively for the benefit of the church, and does not confer grace on the individual ordained. And, happily, it is not only possible, but very easy, to do this.

For we have only to conclude, as we most reasonably may, that our church considers that the grace of which she speaks, in the language adverted to, be it of what kind or character it may, "makes" (we are using her own language) "for the edification of Christ's church," and not for that of the individual ordained, in order to reconcile this apparent inconsistency in the most satisfactory manner.

For instance, when 'holiness' is said by our church to be an effect of ordination; if we conclude (as we most reasonably may) that our church thereby intends that ordination—'the ordination, let us say, for argument's sake, of a wicked individual'—conduces to the sanctification or 'holiness' of the faithful believer, by enabling the individual, so ordained, to minister—to bless (let us say) in the name of the Lord, with a mysterious efficacy which would have been wanting if he had not been apostolically ordained, and, at his ordination, received an unction of the Holy Spirit for the benefit of the church, we shall perceive, that 'holiness' may very consistently be said to be an effect of ordination, at the same time that ordination is holden to operate exclusively for the benefit of the church.

And supposing, for the sake of argument, that any one should conceive that he has just cause to conclude that the expression 'holiness,' or any other which appears to intimate that ordination conveys some description or degree of personal grace, must be considered to apply to the individual ordained;

in that case, be it observed, our statement that, 'according to the orthodox system of the Church of England, ordination is a sacred commission of Christ's institution, which is attended with an unction of the Holy Spirit, that operates exclusively for the benefit of the church, but does not confer grace upon the individual,' will not be disproved; nay, it would not be disproved in the event of such a conclusion being right. For all that would be fairly established, in the case supposed, would be this: that our church is chargeable with inconsistency, when she theoretically teaches that ordination confers some description and degree of personal grace upon the individual ordained, at the same time that she practically holds (as we have seen that she does), that the grace bestowed at ordination operates exclusively for the benefit of the church.

No. 3.

We feel called upon to observe, that, in the tract No. 17, and elsewhere, the authors of the Oxford Tracts distinctly state, that "the powers and graces" conferred upon a priest at ordination, are so conferred, as "a trust from Christ, for the benefit of his people."

But the admission of this fact will not weaken, or in any manner affect, our argument. For, supposing it admitted, there will still remain a specific irreconcileable difference betwixt the doctrine holden by the orthodox system of the Church of England, and that taught by the system of the authors of the Oxford Tracts, with respect to ordination.

The nature and extent of the difference which will so remain, may be practically exemplified (if we may so speak) by means of the following illustration:—

There subsists, be it observed, a well ascertained and most important distinction betwixt 'a use' and 'a trust,' two creatures of the law.

If lands be granted to A. for life, to the use of B. and his heirs; or to A. and his heirs, to the use of B. for a term of years, and afterwards to the use of the heirs of C. (which forms of expression effect the limitation of a use,) A. would not take either the beneficial ownership, or what is termed the legal estate (the ownership, that is, at law, or in contemplation, or consideration of the law.) In truth, he would not take any interest whatsoever in the lands, under the grant. Yet the grant made to A. as *feoffee* to uses (as the legal phrase is), constitutes the basis, and is, as it were, a necessary means, or medium, for the communication of the estate which passes to the *cestuique* use (to speak in legal phraseology) to B. and his heirs, that is, in the one case, and to B. and the heirs of C. in the other. For if, in the latter of the cases stated, the lands had been granted to B. for a term of years, and afterwards to the heirs of C. (C. being alive) directly, and without the intervention of the grant to A. and his heirs, the heirs of C. would not have taken any estate or interest whatsoever in the lands: and in the former of the two cases stated, because the grant to A. was limited to an estate for life, B. and his heirs will only take an estate commensurate to that grant; and their estate will therefore determine when the seizin (or estate) which constituted its basis, is at an end, by the decease of A.

Moreover, as A., the *feoffee* to uses, has not any interest in the lands, not any estate except the ministerial (if we may so term it) or instrumental one adverted to, and which is sometimes termed, and for the sake of distinction may allowably be designated, a *scintilla juris*, he cannot convey, or in any manner charge or incumber, them; nor will they escheat (or devolve) to the crown, or to the lord, in case he should die without an heir, or be forfeited upon his attainder of felony or treason.

But where lands are granted unto and to the use of A. and his heirs, upon trust for B. and his heirs (by which form of expression 'a trust' is created), although he would not take any beneficial interest in the lands so granted, A. would have the legal estate, or ownership at law. Indeed, so complete would be his ownership in the consideration of the law, that if he conveyed or mortgaged the lands to a bonâ fide purchaser, to one that is, who had no notice that they were subject to a trust, such a conveyance or mortgage would be binding upon the *cestuique* trust (the person beneficially entitled), and effectually transfer them. And so, in case A. (the trustee) should die without an heir, the lands would escheat to the lord at law; and they would be forfeited at law, in case he were attainted of felony or treason.

Now the difference which subsists betwixt the doctrine holden by the orthodox system of the Church of England, and that taught by the system of the authors of the Oxford Tracts, with respect to ordination, (supposing it to be admitted that the powers and graces which ordination confers are considered by the latter as a trust for the benefit of Christ's Church) is precisely analogous to that which has been shewn to subsist betwixt 'a use' and 'a trust.'

For according to the doctrine holden by the orthodox system of the Church of England, which teaches, as we have seen, that 'ordination is a sacred commission which is attended with an unction of the Holy Spirit, that operates for the benefit of the Church, but does not confer grace upon the individual;' the ordained individual is placed in exactly the same relative position with respect to the members of the Church, as that in which the feoffee to uses is placed with respect to his cestuique use. And as, in the one case, the land, with its appurtenances and profits, passes through the feoffee to uses (who is a mere conduit, if we may so speak, but a necessary conduit) to the cestuique use; and therefore the dishonesty or negligence of the feoffee to uses does not in any manner prejudice or affect the estate or possession of the lands granted to his cestuique use: so in the other case, the grace communicated at ordination, together with its blessed influences and effects, passes (if we may so speak) through the priest (who is a mere conduit, but a necessary conduit) to the Church, or brotherhood of faithful believers; and, consequently, the iniquity or carelessness of the priest does not take away or diminish the grace of God's gift conferred, at ordination, on the Church.

Whereas, according to the doctrine holden by the system of the authors of the Oxford Tracts, which teaches 'that ordination is a rite which confers a special description and degree of personal grace upon the individual ordained, in trust for the benefit of Christ's Church,' the individual ordained is placed in exactly the same relative position with respect to the Church, as that in which a trustee is placed with respect to his cestuique trust.

For as, in the one case, the trustee being the legal owner of the land, may (as such legal owner) alienate the land, or dispose of the profits at his pleasure (supposing him to be dishonest), or depreciate the value of the one, or lessen the income of the other, by his want of management and care (supposing him to be negligent); and will thereby deprive the cestuique trust or person beneficially entitled, either entirely or partially (as the case may be) of the benefit which he was intended to take under the grant: so, in the other case, the ordained individual being the personal recipient of the grace communicated at ordination, he may impede the operation of it, or debar himself of the enjoyment of its influences, by a wicked course of life; or, by neglecting it, he may depreciate and disparage the gift that is in him; and he will thereby deprive the members of Christ's Church either entirely or partially, as the case may be, of the benefits that ordination was intended to confer.

CHAPTER IV.

In approaching the difficult and most momentous question of justification, we would observe, in the first place, that it is consequentially only, and not directly, that the false principle adopted by the authors of the Oxford Tracts is operative in producing that difference which will be found to subsist betwixt their system and the orthodox system of our Church, upon the point in question.

The two systems being constituted, the one on the principle of holding the *via media* between the Protestantism spoken of and Popery, and the other upon that of holding the *via media* between Popery and Socinianism, they are led (as we have seen) to adopt different courses, or (in other words) to inculcate dissimilar doctrines with respect to authority. And it is in consequence of their having taken different courses with respect to authority, that they are led, and will be found, to differ upon the momentous point of justification.

Before we enter upon the consideration of the important subject adverted to, it may be advisable to premise, that both the Church of England and the authors of the Oxford Tracts, in common with the Roman Catholics, and with Christians of every church and sect who ascribe any virtue whatsoever to the atonement, agree in a profession and belief that the one oblation of Himself once offered by our Divine Redeemer—the death of the just for the unjust, is the primary cause, the *origo originans* (as it has been appropriately termed) of man's justification before God

And all who agree in this profession and belief, will of necessity concur in holding that an appropriation of the benefits purchased for the human race by our Redeemer's oblation of Himself, or (as it is otherwise termed) a saving interest in the atonement, is necessary to the justification of each individual before God. All, also, who concur in recognizing the necessity of such an appropriation of the benefits purchased for the human race by our Redeemer's oblation of Himself, to the individual, must of course admit, that it can be obtained only by means divinely appointed for the purpose.

And the means divinely appointed for this purpose may be said to constitute the formal cause, or *origo originata*, of man's justification before God.

Now, it is with respect to this point, viz. as to what are the means divinely appointed for the appropriation of the benefits purchased for the human race by our Redeemer's oblation of Himself, to the individual; or, in other words, as to what constitutes the formal cause, or *origo originata*, of man's justification before God, that those who agree in holding the atonement to be the primary cause, or *origo originans* of justification, and (among them) the adherents to the orthodox system of the Church of England, and the advocates for the system of the authors of the Oxford Tracts, differ as regards the doctrine of justification.

Bearing in mind, then, that the orthodox system of the Church of England, and the system of the authors of the Oxford Tracts, agree in holding the atonement to be the *origo originans* of man's justification before God; we propose to enquire,

1st. What is the doctrine holden by the orthodox system of the Church of England, with respect to the means appointed for the appropriation of a saving interest in our Redeemer's atonement to the individual; or (in other words) with respect to the *origo originata* of a responsible Christian's justification before God?

2ndly. What is the doctrine taught by the system of the authors of the Oxford Tracts with respect to the means appointed for the appropriation of a saving interest in our Redeemer's atonement to the individual, or (in other words) with respect to the *origo originata* of a responsible Christian's justification before God?

3rdly. How, and to what extent, the doctrine holden by the two systems with respect to that which constitutes the *origo originata* of justification, differs?

With respect to the first inquiry. In her third Homily, our Church authoritatively declares, " The right and true Christian faith is, not only to believe that Holy Scripture, and all the aforesaid articles* of our faith, are true ; but also to have a sure trust and confidence in God's merciful promises, to be saved from everlasting damnation by Christ : whereof doth follow a loving heart to obey His commandments."

By this faith, "as it is declared in the last sermon," our Church pronounces in her fourth Homily, " we be justified before God."

Now, it is quite impossible, we conceive, for words to indicate a meaning more unequivocally, than those contained in the passages cited from her Homilies, express the decision or opinion of our Church, that the faith spoken of, which is elsewhere termed a " living or lively faith," is the means appointed for the appropriation of a saving interest in our Redeemer's atonement to the individual; and constitutes what we have termed the *origo originata* of man's justification before God. But to proceed.

In the Homilies before referred to, our Church also most distinctly declares that " It is by this lively faith only " (by this faith alone, that is, without any intervention " of our own works either in part or in the whole ") that " we be justified."

---

* That Christ was born of a virgin ; that he fasted forty days and forty nights ; that he wrought all kinds of miracles, declaring himself very God ; that he suffered a most painful death to redeem us from everlasting death ; that he rose again from death the third day ; that he ascended into heaven ; and that he sitteth at the right hand of God, and at the end of the world shall come again to judge both the quick and the dead ;" are the articles of our faith alluded to.

In order to obviate any seeming inconsistency which may be observable betwixt the unequivocal decision which our Church has pronounced in the passages cited from her Homilies, and any expressions made use of in her documents and formularies, which (when inconsiderately appealed to) may appear to intimate a different opinion, we propose to subjoin the following brief exposition of the doctrine which has been shewn to be that which she teaches with respect to justification.

We conceive, then, that by virtue of the Holy Sacrament of Baptism, whereby (as our Church declares) they who are born in sin and the children of wrath, are made the children of grace, and become members of Christ, children of God, and inheritors of the kingdom of heaven; the baptised and regenerate Christian is endued with a measure of that preventing grace, without which " he cannot turn " (as our Church declares) " to faith and calling upon God." *

But man being " very far gone from original righteousness," as our Church also declares,† " and of his own nature inclined to evil, so that the flesh lusteth always contrary to the spirit; and " this infection of nature " remaining (as she asserts that it does) in them that are regenerated, the preventing grace with which the baptised Christian has been endued is resisted by the flesh, by that " infection of

---

* 10th Article. † 9th Article.

nature" which is permitted to remain in the regenerate.

But the baptised and regenerate Christian is not only endued (at baptism) with a measure of preventing grace, which invests him as it were with power to turn to faith, and calling upon God; he is also blessed with the continual assistance or "daily renewal" (as our Church has designated it) of the Holy Spirit, and thereby "incited to turn to faith and calling upon God." But in God's inscrutable wisdom, certain malignant principalities and powers, which are comprehended by our Church under the general appellation of the Devil, are permitted to exert an antagonist evil influence, which opposes itself to that by which the baptized and regenerate Christian is assisted.

And it is, as we conceive, the state in which a baptized Christian is placed, when, being thus endued with baptismal or preventing grace and blessed with the assisting influences of the Holy Spirit, and, at the same time, left subject to that "infection of nature" which is permitted to remain in the regenerate, and exposed to a malignant influence exerted by evil principalities and powers, he is sent forth to act his part in a world of trial and temptation, that constitutes his life—that constitutes the life of every baptized Christian who lives to attain to an age and state of responsibility—that condition of spiritual warfare which it was intended to become.

Now, when engaged in the spiritual warfare which

he is thus called upon to wage, and qualified to carry on, according as the baptized Christian (in what appears to human apprehension to be an exercise of his free will)* refuses the evil and chooses the good, or refuses the good and chooses the evil, he achieves victory or sustains defeat.

In the one case—if the evil be refused and duly resisted in its subsequent aggressions—through the preventing grace with which he has been endued at baptism and the assisting influences of the Holy Spirit, the baptized Christian will insensibly be led towards, and eventually attain unto, that lively faith which our Church holds to be the means appointed for the appropriation of a saving interest in Christ's atonement to the individual, and be justified before God.

In the other—if the good be refused; if forsaking his own mercy by wilfully resisting the preventing grace with which he has been endued, and making light of the assisting influences of the Holy Spirit, the baptized and regenerate Christian yield to the influences of evil, he will be led to that carnal mind which is enmity with God, and constitute himself an enemy in his mind to God and godliness, by wicked works.

Whilst he continues in this state of enmity; nay, even after he has given himself over to work all iniquity with greediness, from God's inconceivably

---

* Vide Justificative Appendix to Chapter IV.

abundant mercy in Christ, and because He who is in the baptized Christian (unless he be reprobate) is greater than he who is in the world, the baptized Christian who has constituted himself an enemy in his mind by wicked works will be visited by convictions of sin, and experience calls to repentance; and, according as he yields to and obeys these convictions of sin and calls to repentance, or resists and makes light of them (as he unhappily may do), he will either be converted from the error of his way, and thereby be placed, as it were, in a position in which he is enabled to renew his spiritual warfare with success, and to attain (if true to himself) to that lively faith which constitutes the *origo originata* of man's justification before God: or, (in the event of his continuing to forsake his own mercy by obstinately persisting in his resistance to the convictions of sin and calls to repentance, by which he may be visited,) the Holy Spirit will at last be withdrawn, and, becoming reprobate, the baptized Christian will be no longer able to turn to faith, and calling upon God, but live fore-ordained or pre-condemned unto perdition.

Now, from the extracts which we have given from the Homilies of our Church, and from the above exposition of the doctrine which they inculcate, it is indisputably evident, that, according to the orthodox system of the Church of England, a lively faith (that true Christian faith of which a loving heart is the inseparable concomitant) attained unto through the grace communicated at baptism, is the means afforded for the appropriation of a saving interest in our Redeemer's atonement to the individual, and constitutes the *origo originata* of a responsible Christian's justification before God.

And now having ascertained, most distinctly (as we trust), what is the doctrine taught by the orthodox system of the Church of England, with respect to the means appointed for the appropriation of a saving interest in our Redeemer's atonement to the individual, we may proceed to inquire,

In the second place, What is the doctrine taught by the system of the authors of the Oxford Tracts, with respect to the means appointed for the appropriation of a saving interest in our Redeemer's atonement to the individual; or (in other words) with respect to the *origo originata* of a responsible Christian's justification before God?

In proceeding to make this inquiry, we cannot (as we conceive) do better than refer to the Lectures upon Justification, delivered, and subsequeutly published, by an eminent Divine who is understood to be one of the principal contributors to the Oxford Tracts.

Upon referring to the Lectures adverted to, we find that the doctrine holden by Mr. Newman, with respect to the point in question, is in substance this: 'That the fulfilment of the law by a man's own doings, performed through a power conferred by the grace communicated at baptism, is the means appointed for the appropriation of a saving interest in our Redeemer's atonement to the individual.'

CHAPTER IV.

That such is the case—that the doctrine inculcated by Mr. Newman, in his Lectures upon Justification, is to the effect stated above, will be indisputably evident upon an impartial and intelligent perusal of the work.

Mr. Newman commences by considering (in his 1st Lecture) what he maintains to be the erroneous doctrine that "faith is the instrument of justification."

In the 2nd Lecture, he proceeds to consider what he calls "the opposite scheme of doctrine, that justification consists in renewal of the Holy Ghost;" and after treating of this scheme of doctrine at considerable length, he comes to the following conclusion—a conclusion, be it observed, which is stated in language as unequivocal as it is possible to use! viz.: " That this doctrine " (the doctrine that 'justification consists in renewal of the Holy Ghost') "is the doctrine concerning our justification, which has the testimony of the whole Christian Church in its favour, and which, I suppose, all sober minds would admit at once, except from some notion that it contradicts our Articles." *

Now, if the passage cited above had stood alone, and were not (as it is) partially contradicted by that which immediately succeeds, we should have been fully authorized to state that the doctrine maintained by Mr. Newman, with respect to justification,

---

* Vide p. 60.

was, 'that it consisted in the renewal of the Holy Ghost.' For since Mr. Newman conceives the doctrine, 'that justification consists in renewal of the Holy Ghost,' to be "one which all sober minds would admit at once, except from a notion that it contradicts our Articles," we may very safely infer that it is one which he himself admits.

The passage referred to as succeeding, and partially contradicting, that last referred to, is the following: " What our Articles add in it, and in what respect it is defective, and how it may be unscripturally used, shall be considered hereafter."

With respect to the first and last of the subjects reserved by Mr. Newman, in the above sentence, for future consideration, viz., "as to what our Articles add in it" (whatever may be the precise meaning of the phrase,) and "how" (like every other doctrine, whether true or false) " it may be unscripturally used," we have no concern; but it is especially incumbent upon us to ascertain in what respect it is that Mr. Newman conceives the doctrine adverted to, to be "defective:" for until we ascertain this, we cannot pretend to determine what is the doctrine which he holds with respect to justification.

But having ascertained in what respect it is that Mr. Newman considers the doctrine, ' that justification consists in renewal of the Holy Ghost,' to be defective; or, in other words, what it is that he holds to be wanting to complete it, we shall be able to determine with certainty what it is that he accounts to be the true doctrine with respect to "our justification."

In continuing our perusal of Mr. Newman's Lectures, with a view of ascertaining this, we find it stated, "That it" (the doctrine that justification consists in the renewal of the Holy Ghost) "is not complete, because St. Augustine and the Fathers go beyond it." *

We must proceed, it is obvious, to ascertain in what respect it is that Mr. Newman conceives that St. Augustine and the Fathers go beyond the doctrine 'that justification consists in the renewal of the Holy Ghost.'

Upon instituting this inquiry, we find that Mr. Newman conceives that St. Augustine goes beyond the doctrine 'that justification consists in the renewal of the Holy Ghost,' by maintaining that it is by, or through the medium of, their own doings—by fulfilling the law, through a power enabling them so to do, communicated by such "renewal of the Holy Ghost," that men are justified before God.

That such is the case—that Mr. Newman conceives that St. Augustine maintains this, will become evident beyond all possibility of doubt, upon a perusal of his 2nd Lecture. Indeed, inasmuch as Mr. Newman has distinctly asserted that St. Augustine maintains that "we are justified only by the Spirit enabling us to fulfil the law,"† we may safely conclude

---

* Vide p. 65.   † Vide p. 55.

that he conceives that St. Augustine maintains the doctrine, 'that it is by fulfilling the law through a power enabling them so to do, communicated by such "renewal of the Holy Ghost," that we are justified,' without being under the necessity of perusing his 2nd Lecture.

Now inasmuch as we have seen that Mr. Newman admits that the doctrine, ' that justification consists in renewal of the Holy Ghost,' is the right doctrine concerning our justification—is " a true doctrine, in the main," as he elsewhere expresses himself, but defective in a certain particular (if we may so speak) ; and intimates, or rather asserts, that that particular is one in which St. Augustine goes beyond it— beyond the doctrine that justification consists in the renewal of the Holy Ghost; and then informs us that St. Augustine goes beyond the doctrine 'that justification consists in the renewal of the Holy Ghost,' by maintaining that 'it is by fulfilling the law by the assistance of the Spirit ; or, in other words, through a power conferred by the renewal of the Holy Ghost, that we are justified ;' we may safely conclude—it is in truth self-evident, that the doctrine holden by Mr. Newman with respect to justification, is in substance such as we have above stated it to be.

It may be predicated, therefore, that according to the system of the authors of the Oxford Tracts, 'The fulfilment of the law by a man's own doings, performed through a power conferred by the grace communicated at baptism, is the means appointed for the appropriation of a saving interest in our Redeemer's atonement to the individual, and constitutes the *origo originata* of a responsible Christian's justification before God. Having ascertained this, we may proceed,

In the third place, to inquire how and to what extent the doctrine respectively holden by the two systems adverted to, with regard to the *origo originata* of a responsible Christian's justification, differs?

To place them in juxta-position is all that will be necessary to convince us that they differ irreconcileably. Let us proceed to do this.

According to the orthodox system of the Church of England.	*According to the system of the authors of the Oxford Tracts.*
"A lively faith attained unto through the grace communicated at baptism—and faith, this lively faith, only—is the means appointed for the appropriation of a saving interest in our Redeemer's atonement to the individual, and constitutes the *origo originata* of a responsible Christian's justification before God."	"The fulfilment of the law by a man's own doings, performed through a power conferred by the grace communicated at baptism, is the means appointed for the appropriation of a saving interest in our Redeemer's atonement to the individual, and constitutes the *origo originata* of a responsible Christian's justification before God."

With a view, however, of rendering the illimitable extent (for such we most assuredly may term it) of the difference which obtains betwixt the above doctrines, or systems of doctrine, more practically manifest, we propose to lay down and establish (as we trust) the following position.

That the character of the Christian religion—the very spirit and genius (if we may so speak) of Christianity—will radically differ according as the one or the other of them is true.

If the doctrine holden by the orthodox system of the Church of England be true—if it be true that a lively faith attained unto through the grace communicated at baptism, is the means appointed for the appropriation of a saving interest in our Redeemer's atonement to the individual—it may truly be predicated of the Christian religion, that "her ways are ways of pleasantness, and that all her paths are peace," it may truly be affirmed that our Saviour's yoke is easy, and his burthen light; it may easily be made manifest, that Christian godliness has the promise of the life that now is, as well as of that which is to come.

Whereas, if the doctrine taught by the system of the Authors of the Oxford Tracts be true,—if it be true that the fulfilment of the law by a man's own doings, performed through a power conferred by the grace communicated at baptism, is the means divinely appointed for the appropriation of a saving interest in our Redeemer's atonement to the individual—it cannot be predicated of the Christian religion that her ways are ways of pleasantness, and that her paths are peace: neither can it be truly affirmed that our Saviour's yoke is easy and his burthen light; nor made manifest that Christian godliness has the promise of the life that now is, as well as of that which is to come. But in that case—supposing the doctrine taught by the system of the Authors of the Oxford Tracts to be true—the truth of the converse of these several positions may be indisputably established.

'The above startling assertions remain to be proved;' it will doubtless be observed. We will proceed to support them to the best of our ability. With a view of doing so, we would observe, in the first place:

That if the doctrine which we have shewn to be that holden by the orthodox system of the Church of England be true—if a lively faith, a faith of which a loving heart to keep God's commandments is the inseparable concomitant, attained unto through the grace communicated at baptism, be, and be believed to be, the means divinely appointed for the appropriation of a saving interest in our Redeemer's atonement to the individual,' it will be practicable for every sincere believer to attain to an assurance that he is in a justified state—in a state, that is, in which, if he died upon the instant, he would escape eternal perdition.

For a loving heart to keep God's commandments being (as it will be in the case supposed) the inseparable concomitant of a true and lively faith, it follows that every sincere believer, every one who possesses a true and lively faith, will also possess that loving heart which is its inseparable concomitant: and one who really possesses a loving heart to keep God's commandments may, upon duly instituting an inquiry into his spiritual condition, become conscious that he possesses it for such an inquiry; will resolve itself into a simple question of fact: and having become conscious that he possesses that loving heart to keep God's commandments which is the inseparable concomitant of that true and lively faith which he believes to be the means divinely appointed for the appropriation of a saving interest in our Redeemer's atonement to the individual, he of whom we speak will have the witness in himself, that he possesses that true and lively faith which is the means appointed for the appropriation of a saving interest in our Redeemer's atonement to the individual, and thus attain to an assurance that he is in a justified state.*

That joy and peace in believing must be a necessary consequence of such an assurance, is indisputably evident.

Again: if the doctrine that a lively faith, a faith of which a loving heart to keep God's commandments, is the inseparable concomitant, attained unto through the grace communicated at baptism, is the means divinely appointed for the appropriation of a saving interest in our Redeemer's atonement to the individual, be true, communion with God; religious meditation; joy in the Lord; a thankful sense of his goodness; a hearty resignation to his will; the consideration of his ways (reflections on God's providence, that is) and the contemplation of his works (all of which are

---

* Vide Appendix No. 2.

exercises or employments that constitute important and acceptable duties, at the same time that they afford the highest and most rational satisfaction of which man's present condition is susceptible) will be the most efficacious, and may be regarded as the principal, means of promoting an advance in godliness.

For the employments or exercises adverted to, have a natural, direct, and powerful tendency to increase and strengthen faith—constitute, in fact, the most efficacious means of strengthening and increasing faith; and with the strength and increase of faith, that loving heart to keep God's commandments which is its inseparable concomitant, will receive a proportional increase in vivacity and fervour. And this increase in faith and proportionately augmented fervour in the loving heart to keep God's commandments, which is its inseparable concomitant, will necessarily conduce to an advance in practical godliness.

And as a recourse to the employments or exercises adverted to; or the practice, let us say, of the duties of which the performance affords the highest and most rational satisfaction of which man's present condition is susceptible, will necessarily conduce to the believer's advance in godliness (in the case supposed); so the believer's advance in godliness will naturally lead to their more frequent use; and their more frequent use will in turn facilitate and give increased efficiency to their future employment. "For as"—to use the language of an excellent old divine who has expressed himself to much the same effect—

"as an holy behaviour, and the use of God's blessings, dispose us unto prayer, meditation, and such like duties: so prayer again requites them, and returns the kindness upon their own heads, by disposing and preparing us for such like holy deportment for the future. Prayer, &c., makes a Christian live holily, and a holy life makes us fit to pray fervently. And both the one and the other are not only parts of our duty, which God commands, but instruments and helps to doing our duty. Such a combination there is between all the things that God requires, to make them easy and familiar, desirable and pleasant."*

Once more: as the doctrine which we have shewn to be that holden by the orthodox system of the Church of England, is calculated to fill the baptized Christian who has attained unto a lively faith, with joy and peace in believing: so, it is replete with encouragement and hope to the sinner, to a baptized Christian, who has forsaken his own mercy so far as to constitute himself an enemy in his mind by wicked works.

Let us suppose that a baptized Christian, who has so far forsaken his own mercy as to have given himself over to work all iniquity with greediness, is brought to reflect seriously on his spiritual condition, and led, in consequence, to inquire what he must do to be saved.

Now if the doctrine, 'that a lively faith attained

---

* Vide Bishop Patrick's Mensa Mystica.

unto through the grace communicated at baptism, is the means divinely appointed for the appropriation of a saving interest in our Redeemer's atonement to the individual,' be announced to and believed by such an one, what is the effect which that announcement would have upon him? or rather, what is the effect which it is calculated to produce?

Being sensible (as the individual of whom we speak would necessarily be) that he is a baptized Christian; and conceiving (as such an one might reasonably do, from the circumstances of his having experienced and been influenced by the serious impression we have supposed him to act under,) that he had not become reprobate; he of whom we speak would be led to conclude—might legitimately conclude—that notwithstanding the number and heinousness of the sins which he may have committed in the past time of his life, he is still in a state of grace—still in a state in which, through that grace of which he was made the unconscious recipient at his baptism, and is still the blessed possessor, he may yet attain unto that lively faith which is the means divinely appointed for the appropriation of a saving interest in our Redeemer's atonement to the individual, and be justified before God.

It is surely needless to point out how full of hope and encouragement such a conviction must inevitably be; or how powerful will be the effect which it must necessarily have in stimulating the sinner to seek the things which belong unto his peace with full purpose of heart—to seek so that he shall find, and to knock so that it may be opened to him!

Now if the case be thus—if (supposing the doctrine which we have seen to be that holden by the orthodox system of the Church of England be true) every sincere believer who is not precluded from doing so by any natural or accidental impediment, may attain to an assurance that he is in a justified state, and will, in consequence, experience a joy and peace in believing; and if (in the case supposed) certain exercises or employments which constitute important and acceptable duties, at the same time that they afford the highest and most rational satisfaction of which man's present condition is susceptible, will supply the most efficacious, and must be regarded as the principal, means of promoting an advance in godliness; and if the doctrine in question is replete with encouragement and hope to the sinner, and has the effect of powerfully stimulating him to seek the things which belong unto his peace; it will follow— it must be granted, that supposing the doctrine which we have shewn to be that holden by the orthodox system of the Church of England, be true, it may safely be predicated of the Christian religion, that her ways are ways of pleasantness, and her paths peace : it may truly be affirmed that our Saviour's yoke is easy and his burthen light; it will be abundantly manifest that Christian godliness has the promise of the life that now is, as well as of that which is to come.

But supposing that the doctrine which we have shewn to be that taught by the system of the Authors of the Oxford Tracts be true and be believed—if the fulfilment of the law,* by a man's own doings performed through a power conferred by the grace communicated at baptism, be, and be believed to be, the means divinely appointed for the appropriation of a saving interest in our Redeemer's atonement to the individual, it will be impracticable for any man to attain to a well founded assurance that he is in a justified state—that he is in a state in which, if he died upon the instant, he would escape eternal perdition.

For an "infection of nature" consequent upon the fall of man having been permitted to remain " in them that are regenerated,"† in men, that is, after they have been endued with the grace which the sacrament of baptism communicates, it is obviously impossible that any man, even when endued with the power conferred by the grace communicated at baptism, can fulfil the pure and holy law of God. And if it be impracticable for any man to fulfil the law, notwithstanding he is endued with the grace communicated at baptism, it will of course be impossible for him to attain to a rational and abiding conviction that he does fulfil it. And if it be impossible for such an one to

---

* Vide Appendix, No. 3.

† The doctrine to this effect asserted by our Church in her IXth Article, is not denied by the Authors of the Oxford Tracts.

arrive at a conviction that he fulfils the law, it must necessarily be impracticable for him to attain to an assurance that he is in a justified state, supposing that the fulfilment of the law by a man's own doings, performed through a power conferred by the grace communicated at baptism, be, and be believed to be, the means divinely appointed for the appropriation of a saving interest in our Redeemer's atonement to the individual.

Now without some such assurance as that of which we speak, it is quite impossible for any man to experience a settled joy and peace in believing. Indeed it is indisputably evident that in the case supposed—if it be impossible for any one to attain to a well founded assurance that he is in a justified state, the more religious any man became—the more his thoughts and affections were set upon the things that are unseen and eternal—the more anxious and miserable he must necessarily be.

Again: if it be true and be believed ' that the fulfilment of the law by a man's own doings, through a power conferred by the grace communicated at baptism, is the means divinely appointed for the appropriation of a saving interest in our Redeemer's atonement to the individual,' the practice of rigorous mortification and austerities will constitute the most efficacious, and must be regarded as the principal means of promoting an advance in godliness.

For "an infection of nature" being permitted (as we have seen) to remain in them that are regenerated, in men, nothwithstanding their endowment with baptismal grace; when one who is earnest in seeking the things which belong unto his peace, and with a view of employing the means which he considers to be those divinely appointed for the appropriation of a saving interest in our Redeemer's atonement to the individual, endeavours to fulfil the perfect law of God, he will inevitably find himself foiled in the attempt. And upon being thus foiled in his attempt to fulfil the law, he of whom we speak—one who believes the doctrine 'that the fulfilment of the law by a man's own doings, performed through a power conferred by the grace communicated at baptism, is the means divinely appointed for the appropriation of a saving interest in our Redeemer's atonement to the individual,' must become conscious that he does not duly employ the means appointed for the appropriation of a saving interest in our Redeemer's atonement to the individual, and is not therefore in a justified state—in a state in which, if he died upon the instant, he would enter into life.

Now to one who is in the fearful predicament adverted to—to one who is conscious of the failure of his most strenuous endeavours to fulfil the perfect law of God, in consequence of the obstruction which he meets with from his fallen nature, at the same time that he believes that the fulfilment of the law by a man's own doings is the means divinely appointed for the appropriation of a saving interest in our Redeemer's atonement to the individual; the practice of rigorous mortification and austerities would present itself as the most available means of enabling him to remove the obstructions (if we may so speak) which cause or mainly contribute to the defeat of his attempts to fulfil the perfect law of God; and appear, therefore, to constitute, and be regarded as, the principal and most efficacious means—and supposing the doctrine taught by the Authors of the Oxford Tracts were true, they would actually be the principal and most efficacious means—of promoting an advance in godliness.*

And be it observed that that "infection of nature" consequent upon the Fall, which has been permitted to remain in them that are regenerated, being the cause of man's inability to fulfil the perfect law of God, it is evident that the practice of the most rigorous mortifications and austerities to which it is possible to resort, must necessarily prove insufficient to enable a man to compass the fulfilment of the law; and consequently, in spite of a recourse to the greatest possible endurable mortification and austerity, one who believes 'that the fulfilment of the law, by a man's own doings, is the means divinely appointed for the appropriation of a saving interest in our Redeemer's atonement to the individual,' and endeavours to fulfil the law with a view of employing the means so appointed for the appropriation of a

---

* Vide Appendix, No 4.

saving interest in our Redeemer's atonement to the individual, will, of necessity, find himself foiled in his attempt; and being conscious, in consequence, that he has not obtained a saving interest in our Redeemer's atonement, he must inevitably remain subject to a tormenting fear of eternal perdition.

Once more: the doctrine, 'that the fulfilment of the law, by a man's own doings, performed through a power conferred by the grace communicated at baptism, is the means divinely appointed for the appropriation of a saving interest in our Redeemer's atonement to the individual,' has a tendency to discourage the self-convicted sinner, and is but too well calculated to drive him to despair.

For supposing it to be announced to, and believed by, a baptized Christian, who, after having forsaken his own mercy so far as to have given himself over to work all iniquity with greediness, is brought to reflect seriously upon his spiritual condition, and led, in consequence, to ask what he must do to be saved: what is the effect which such an announcement is calculated to produce?

Being sensible (as such an one will necessarily be) that, as a baptized Christian, he has been endued with a power enabling him to fulfil the law; and conscious that (notwithstanding his baptismal endowment with this power) he had given himself over to work all iniquity with greediness, and submitted to the dominion of evil habits and propensities, in place of availing himself of it, to fulfil the law, and secure that appropriation of a saving interest in our Redeemer's atonement, which is necessary to his justification; and being aware (as such one must be) that, by so giving himself over to work all iniquity with greediness, and submitting to the dominion of evil habits and propensities, he had voluntarily rendered the object for which he had been endowed with the power conferred by the communication of baptismal grace (the fulfilment of the law) of incalculably more difficult attainment, than it would otherwise have been; whilst, by his long neglect and disuse of it, the power so conferred by the communication of baptismal grace had become of less efficiency, or rather less available (less serviceable, that is, to him); he of whom we speak would find himself in a situation analogous to that of one who, with the little strength that remained to him in a season of sickness and old age, was called upon to contend with adversaries by whom he had been worsted in the vigour of his youth, and at a time when they were incalculably less potent than they are at present.

And that this,—that finding himself in a situation thus obviously and most closely analogous to that of one who, in sickness and old age, has to contend with adversaries who had worsted him when he was in the vigour of his youth, and they less potent than at present,—must greatly discourage the self-convicted sinner of whom we speak, and is but too likely to drive him to despair, is undeniably certain.

Now if the case be thus—if (supposing the doctrine, 'that the fulfilment of the law, by a man's own doings, performed through a power conferred by the grace communicated at baptism, is the means divinely appointed for the appropriation of a saving interest in our Redeemer's atonement to the individual,' be true) it must of necessity be impracticable for any man to attain to a well-founded assurance that he is in a justified state: and if (in the case supposed) the practice of rigorous mortification and austerities will constitute the most efficacious, and must be regarded as the principal, means of promoting an advance in godliness; and since, as we have seen, the doctrine in question has a tendency to discourage the self-convicted sinner, and is but too well calculated to drive him to despair; it will follow—it must be granted, that supposing the doctrine taught by the system of the Authors of the Oxford Tracts be true, it cannot be predicated of the Christian religion, that her ways are ways of pleasantness, and her paths peace—neither can it be truly affirmed, that our Saviour's yoke is easy, and his burthen light; nor made manifest that Christian godliness, hath the promise of the life that now is, as well as of that which is to come.

And moreover: since it is undeniable that if it be impossible for any one to attain to a well-founded assurance that he is in a justified state, the more religious a man becomes, the more his thoughts and affections are set upon the things that are unseen and eternal, the more anxious and miserable he must necessarily be; and evident (as we have seen), that if the doctrine, that ' the fulfilment of the law by a man's own doings, performed through a power conferred by the grace communicated at baptism, is the means divinely appointed for the appropriation of a saving interest in our Redeemer's atonement to the individual' be true, it must necessarily be impossible for any man to attain to such an assurance: and inasmuch as, if the doctrine adverted to, be true and be believed, it must have the effect (as we have shewn) of subjecting men to a tormenting fear of eternal perdition, because from that " infection of nature," which has been permitted to remain in the regenerate, men are unable to fulfil the perfect law of God, and must, therefore, be conscious that they do not employ the means divinely appointed for the appropriation of a saving interest in our Redeemer's atonement to the individual (supposing the doctrine adverted to, be true and be believed): and because (as we have seen) the doctrine adverted to has a tendency to discourage the self-convicted sinner, and is but too well calculated to drive him to despair: it follows—it must be granted, that if the doctrine taught by the system of the Oxford Tracts be true, the converse of the several positions maintainable, supposing the doctrine holden by the orthodox system of the Church of England be true; viz., that the ways of the Christian religion are ways of wretchedness and anxiety; that our Saviour's yoke is galling, and his burthen heavy;

and that whatever may be the promise which Christian godliness may have, as to the life to come, it has no promise as to the life that now is; must be admitted to be tenable.*

JUSTIFICATIVE APPENDIX TO CHAP. IV.

THE author conceives that there is no "certainty of reason" more evident than this: viz., that the most mysterious subject to which it has become necessary for him thus briefly to advert, is one which it has pleased God to place without the range of the human intellect: and that, in consequence, any attempt to reason upon the question, 'whether that which appears to human apprehension to be an exercise of man's free will is, or can be properly such,' must of necessity be dangerously presumptuous.

That some such action of what appears to human apprehension to be man's free will, as that to which we advert, is essential to the attainment of a justifying faith, or to the attainment (in other words) of a state in which the righteousness of God is upon imperfect, and therefore (in the strict sense of the word) unrighteous man, is maintained, as we conceive, by St. Augustine, in the following passages; which, (with a different interpretation placed upon them) are referred to by Mr. Newman,† in support of the view which he has taken of the subject under discussion.

"Sine voluntate tuâ non erit in te justitia Dei. Esse potest justitia Dei sine voluntate tuâ, sed in te esse non potest præter voluntatem tuam."

It is with unfeigned satisfaction, be it observed, that we

---

* Vide Appendix, No. 5.
† Vide Lectures on Justification, p. 111.

fortify the statement of our views, upon the most momentous point adverted to above, by the authority of St. Augustine—an authority which we consider entitled to the greatest possible weight, as against, or in favour of the private opinion of an individual; at the same time that we hold it to be inadmissible, as against, or in favour of any decision of our church.

It may possibly be contended, that, according to the statement given above, we make human merit a participant (if we may so speak) in man's justification before God.

Let us suppose that a benevolent individual had provided some good gift for a destitute beggar, to whose frame he had restored animation, as it lay in a state of insensibility, and freely proffers it to him: now when the beggar raises his hand—that hand to which motion has been restored by his benefactor, to receive the gift thus freely proffered to him, would there be merit in that act? It is true that we may say, 'that there would be merit in that act;' for we may call "darkness, light; and light, darkness;" or "bitter, sweet; and sweet, bitter;" if we think proper to use words at our own arbitrary will and pleasure. But if we use the word 'merit,' according to its authorized and legitimate acceptation, as signifying 'deserving of reward,' can we say that there would be merit in the act of one who raised his hand to receive a gift offered to him under the circumstances adverted to? There might—there would be, we immediately perceive, egregious folly, and astonishing infatuation in the refusal of such an one to raise his hand to receive the good gift which was freely proffered to him; but there could not possibly be merit, in the legitimate signification of the word, in his raising his hand to receive, or giving any other indication of a purpose to accept, the proffered gift.

Now the case is precisely the same with respect to the mysterious act of the will, of which we speak.

For our blessed Redeemer has effected that for man which we have supposed a benevolent individual to have done for a destitute beggar to whose frame he had restored animation as it lay in a state of insensibility. He has provided a good gift for man—the unspeakable blessing of justification unto life, and restored him to a state in which he is capable of availing himself of it. And through the preventing grace communicated at baptism, and the assisting influences of the Holy Spirit, and by the instrumentality (in most cases) of various providential dispensations, he leads and incites the baptized and regenerate Christian unto faith, and thus proffers (as it were) the good gift which he has provided. And although there may be—there most undoubtedly is—egregious folly and astonishing infatuation in the conduct of the baptized Christian who neglects or refuses to exert that mysterious act or exercise of the will which is necessary to his attainment unto faith, or to a reception, in other words, of the good gift proffered by our Redeemer: yet there is not, there cannot possibly be, ' merit,' in the authorized and legitimate sense of the word, in the conduct of that baptized Christian who exerts such mysterious act or exercise of the will, and thereby accepts the good gift which has been *provided for*, and *proffered to*, him by one to whose good offices he owes *the power of accepting it*, which he possesses.

No. 2.

It is true, it may be advisable to remark, that although, if the doctrine ' that a lively faith—a faith of which a loving heart to keep God's commandments is the inseparable concomitant—is the means divinely appointed for the appropriation of a saving interest in our Redeemer's atonement to the individual,' be true, the assurance of which we speak must, of necessity, be attainable by every sincere believer, it may not be, in all cases, actually attained. For certain natural and accidental impediments—a morbid state of mind, for instance, or erroneous views—may have the effect of precluding a sincere believer from attaining to it.

But in every such case, be it observed, it is by the operation of an extraneous influence, from causes purely accidental, that the believer is precluded from attaining to the assurance of which we speak.

And but for such extrinsic influence—supposing that there were not any such unfavourable extrinsic influence in operation, it would be practicable for every one who is possessed of that lively faith of which a loving heart is the inseparable concomitant, to arrive at a consciousness that he possesses it; and to attain, in consequence, to an assurance, that he is in a justified state, supposing that the doctrine, that 'a lively faith attained unto through the grace communicated at baptism, is the means divinely appointed for the appropriation of a saving interest in our Redeemer's atonement to the individual,' be true.

No. 3.

It may be advisable to remark, that supposing it be contended —nay, granting, for the sake of argument, that it could be fairly established, that Mr. Newman did not mean to maintain (as we have seen that he virtually does) 'that the fulfilment of the law by a man's own doings, performed through a power conferred through the grace communicated at baptism, is the means divinely appointed for the appropriation of a saving interest in our Redeemer's atonement to the individual;' but only intended to assert 'that a man's own doings performed in fulfilment of the law,' or, in other words, that a partial fulfilment of the law, was the means appointed for the appropriation of a saving interest in our Redeemer's atonement to the individual, and constituted the *origo originata* of justification: yet the circumstance of the fulfilment of the law intended by Mr. Newman, being a partial instead of a complete one, will not have the effect of in any degree weakening the force of our observations as to the tendency which the doctrine taught by the system of the Authors of the Oxford Tracts, with respect to the *origo originata* of justification, has to communicate a character of repulsiveness to Christianity.

For supposing 'a man's own doings performed in partial fulfilment of the law,' to be the means divinely appointed for the appropriation of a saving interest in our Redeemer's atonement to the individual, it would still be equally impracticable for any man to attain to an assurance that he is in a justified state, inasmuch as he would have no means of satisfactorily ascertaining what quantum, if we may so speak, of his own doings would be sufficient to constitute an adequate partial fulfilment of the law—a partial fulfilment of the law, that is, sufficient to secure an appropriation of a saving interest in the atonement.

And so again: if 'a man's own doings, performed in partial fulfilment of the law, were the means divinely appointed for the appropriation of a saving interest in our Redeemer's atonement to the individual,' the practice of rigorous mortification and austerities would continue to constitute and must still be regarded as the principal and most efficacious means of promoting an advance in godliness; for not having any means of satisfying himself that he had done enough in partial fulfilment of the law to secure an appropriation of a saving interest in the atonement, a man could not arrive at a rational and abiding conviction that he duly employed the means divinely appointed for the appropriation of a saving interest in our Redeemer's atonement, and would therefore remain subject to a tormenting fear of eternal perdition, and be goaded by it to the practice of rigorous mortification and austerities; which he would continue to regard as the principal and most efficacious means of removing the obstructions by which his attempts to compass what he regarded as an adequate partial fulfilment of the law had hitherto been foiled.

The doctrine also, that a ' man's own doings, performed in partial fulfilment of the law, are the means appointed for the appropriation of a saving interest in our Redeemer's atonement to the individual,' will have a tendency to discourage and depress the spiritual energies of a self-convicted sinner; although it may not (and will not, we admit) have as direct and powerful an one, or be so likely to drive the sinner to despair, as the doctrine which makes the means appointed for the appropriation of a saving interest in our Redeemer's atonement to consist in " the fulfilment of the law."

No. 4.

As the branch of our argument, to which these observations refer, involves the consideration of a subject to which frequent allusion has been made, in the course of the various controversies to which the publication of the Oxford Tracts has given rise: viz., the practice of mortification and austerities;

we are induced to consider it more in detail than we could conveniently do in the text.

Be it observed, then; that if the doctrine taught by the system of the Authors of the Oxford Tracts, with respect to the *origo originata* of justification be true, the practice of mortification and austerities will (as we have seen) constitute the principal and most efficacious means of promoting an advance in godliness; whilst communion with God (except in deprecatory prayer), religious meditation, and the other employments or exercises adverted to, will, it is evident, be of little or no avail—will be means, in fact, to which it is impossible to resort effectually, because they can be effectually resorted to only by those who are influenced by that " spirit of adoption " which would not, which could not be possessed by any man, if the doctrine adverted to were true.

Whereas, if the doctrine holden by the orthodox system of the Church of England, with respect to the *origo originata* of justification be true, the case will be exactly, or very nearly, reversed—then, communion with God, religious meditation, and the other employments or exercise adverted to, will constitute the principal and most efficacious means of promoting an advance in godliness; whilst the practice of mortification and austerities will be but of occasional necessity and a subordinate utility.

But we will proceed, as we proposed to do, to treat the subject of the practice of mortification, somewhat more in detail.

When, then, before he attained unto a lively faith, the baptized Christian had so far forsaken his own mercy as to have given himself over to work all iniquity with greediness, and had subjected himself to the dominion of evil habits and propensities, during many years (it may be) of the past time of his life; a recourse to the practice of mortification and austerities will be in the highest degree advisable and expedient—nay, may be said to be necessary (if we use the word in the secondary and popular sense in which it is frequently employed). But the practice of mortification and austerities will be necessary in the case of which we speak, simply because the baptized Christian who has forsaken his own mercy and given himself over to work all iniquity with greediness, will be grievously harassed and beset by the evil habits and propensities to the dominion of which he has voluntarily subjected himself in the past time of his life, and will feel the plague of that aggravated and more inveterate corruption of his nature, which has been superinduced by his sinful course of life: and when resorted to, it will constitute one of the divinely appointed means of convincing the sinner that it is " an evil thing and bitter, to have forsaken the Lord his God."

And so where a baptized Christian has forsaken his own mercy so far as to constitute himself an enemy in his mind by wicked works, although he may not have proceeded so far as to work all iniquity with greediness, upon attaining unto a lively faith he will find a certain degree of mortification and austerity very advisable and expedient, though he may not feel himself constrained to resort to the extremely rigorous observances which those who have given themselves over to work all iniquity with greediness will be under the necessity of adopting.

But where the baptized Christian has attained unto a lively faith without having forsaken his own mercy so far as to constitute himself an enemy in his mind by wicked works, a resort to the practice of mortification and austerities will not be necessary to his spiritual well-being.

In such a case, indeed, a resort to the practice of a judicious and reasonable, but resolute, self-denial will be in the highest degree expedient and advisable, and may be said to be necessary, because of that "infection of nature" which has been permitted to remain " in them that are regenerated," and by which men continue affected in a greater or less degree, after they have attained unto a lively faith, and so long indeed as they continue in the flesh.

But the practice of this self-denial will not (in general*) partake of the character of mortification—will not have that effect of making a man's life bitter unto him, which consti-

---

* We say " in general," because the influence of certain extraneous and accidental causes may have the effect of producing a different result from that of which we speak.

tutes, as we conceive, the essential character of mortification—when resorted to by one who has attained unto a lively faith—that faith of which a loving heart to keep God's commandments is the inseparable concomitant,—without having forsaken his own mercy so far as to constitute himself an enemy in his mind by wicked works. Nay, certain observances, which are not outwardly distinguishable from those in which the most ascetic austerities are practised, will in no respect partake of the character of mortification, when resorted to by one who has attained unto a lively faith without having forsaken his own mercy, in the genuine spirit of Christian liberty.

Supposing, for instance, that a baptized Christian who has attained unto a lively faith—that faith, be it observed, of which a loving heart to keep God's commandments is the inseparable concomitant, without having forsaken his own mercy so far as to constitute himself an enemy in his mind by wicked works; and who lives, let us say, in the habitual employment of the exercises unto godliness to which we have elsewhere adverted; is led to believe, or has found from experience, that fasting is likely to have, or has (as the case may be) a favourable influence upon him, and may have, or has, the effect of furthering his advance in godliness—fasting will become an acceptable observance to him—an obervance to which he will freely and gladly resort, and which he will perform as a labour of love, and therefore with gratification and alacrity.

And the case is the same with respect to other observances: when resorted to by one who has attained unto a lively faith without having forsaken his own mercy, in the spirit of Christian liberty, and performed as labours of love, they will not partake of the character of mortification, although they may exactly resemble those observances in which the most rigorous mortification is practised, in externals and as to appearance.

The cause, we may observe (in subjoining a few brief explanatory remarks, as we deem it advisable to do), why the observances of which we speak, will, in a certain degree, partake of the character of, or constitute, mortification, when resorted to by those who attain unto a lively faith after having forsaken their own mercy so far as to constitute themselves enemies in their minds by wicked works, is, as we conceive, this : Such persons cannot, and do not, resort to the observances of which we speak, in the genuine spirit of Christian liberty, but are constrained to do so by a necessity which they have laid upon themselves.

In the exercise, we would also remark, of the same genuine spirit of Christian liberty in which he has adopted and performs the observances of which we speak, the baptized Christian who has attained unto a lively faith without having forsaken his own mercy, will (if he see fit) dispense with and discontinue them.

We read of a good man who discontinued the practice of fasting because he found that it had a tendency to increase an acerbity of temper to which he was constitutionally liable. And this is exactly the principle, if we may so speak, upon which the baptized Christian who has attained unto a lively faith without having forsaken his own mercy, will habitually act in dispensing with the observances of which we speak in the exercise of that same genuine spirit of Christian liberty in which they were resorted to, when and as he sees fit.

As some confusion may possibly attach to our statements upon the important subject under consideration, which is in some degree attributable (we are willing to flatter ourselves) to the circumstance that, whilst an essential difference will be found to obtain, with respect to the practice of mortification and austerities, according as the doctrine holden by the orthodox system of the Church of England, or that taught by the system of the Authors of the Oxford Tracts, with respect to the *origo originata* of justification, is true ; an accidental one will also be superinduced, according as those who have attained unto a lively faith, have, or have not, forsaken their own mercy so far as to constitute themselves enemies in their minds through wicked works. We avail ourselves of the following illustration, in the hope of elucidating them.

In consequence of " that infection of nature" which has been permitted to remain in the regenerate, the Christian's advance in godliness is as the course of a ship—of a vessel of burthen, that is, against the stream.

And if the doctrine taught by the system of the Authors of the Oxford Tracts with respect to the *origo originata* of justification—the doctrine ' that the fulfilment of the law by a man's own doings, performed through a power conferred by the grace communicated at baptism, is the means appointed for the appropriation of a saving interest in our Redeemer's atonement to the individual,' be true; in order to advance in godliness the baptized Christian will be constrained (as we have seen) to have recourse to the practice of rigorous mortification and austerities: just as mariners who endeavoured to propel their ship against a stream, when unassisted by the wind, would be under the necessity of resorting to the most wearisome and painful labour.

Whereas if the doctrine holden by the orthodox system of the Church of England, with respect to the *origo originata* of justification—the doctrine ' that a lively faith, a faith of which a loving heart to keep God's commandments is the inseparable concomitant, attained unto through the grace communicated at baptism, is the means appointed for the appropriation of a saving interest in our Redeemer's atonement to the individual,' be true; the baptized Christian who has attained unto a lively faith, will find in that loving heart which is its inseparable concomitant, a principle, if we may so speak, which will possess the same influence, or operate, let us say, in the same manner, in his behalf, as a fair wind does in favour of the crew whose vessel stems the current of a stream.

And just as the mariners of a ship that stems the current of a stream by the aid of a propitious breeze, may have duties to perform which might, perhaps, have been dispensed with if they had had but to glide down the stream, instead of to oppose its current; yet they will not be under the necessity of resorting to that wearisome and painful labour which would devolve upon those who attempted to propel their vessel against the current of a stream when unassisted by the wind: so, although the baptized Christian who has attained unto a lively faith, and possesses that loving heart to keep God's commandments which is its inseparable concomitant, will find himself under the necessity of exerting a self-denial, in prosecuting his advance in godliness, which might, possibly, have been dispensed with if the Almighty had seen fit not to permit an " infection of nature " to remain in the regenerate : yet he will not find himself under the necessity of having recourse to the practice of that mortification and austerity to which those who attempt to advance in godliness, unanimated, if we may so speak, by that loving heart which is the inseparable concomitant of a lively faith, will find themselves constrained to resort.

The accidental difference with respect to the practice of mortification and austerities, which will be superinduced according as the baptized Christian who has attained unto a lively faith, has or has not forsaken his own mercy in the past time of his life, will be analogous to that which would obtain betwixt the duties or exertions which would devolve upon the crews of two vessels sailing against a stream, one of which was sea-worthy, and had to make her way only against the current of a smooth and tolerably equable stream, whilst the other was in a state in which she refused to answer her helm, and had to contend with the current of a turgid and swollen one.

No. 5.

Lest what we have stated in the section, if we may so term it, of our text to which these observations refer, should otherwise be open to misconstruction, we deem it advisable to subjoin the following explanatory remarks.

We would observe, then, in the first place, that if the doctrine which we have shewn to be that holden by the orthodox system of the Church of England, with respect to the *origo originata* of justification, be true ; pleasantness and peace will be essential characteristics (so to speak) of Christianity, just as cheerfulness and light are essential characteristics of the day.

And as the clouds which occasionally overspread the sky, do not cause any real diminution of the cheerfulness and light which are essential characteristics of the day; but only occasion a transient and partial interruption in the manifestation of that cheerfulness and light to those whom they chance to overshadow: so, that heaviness through manifold temptations, and the sorrow from a sense of his unworthiness, or consciousness of his sinfulness, which occasionally oppress the sincere believer, do not cause any real diminution in the pleasantness and peace which will be essential characteristics of Christianity, if the doctrine holden by the orthodox system of the Church of England be true; but only occasion a partial and temporary interruption of the tempted (tried, that is) or contrite believer's enjoyment of that pleasantness and peace.

Again: a great and very perceptible difference is observable in the manifestation of that cheerfulness and light which are essential characteristics of the day, according as times and seasons, situation, and other circumstances or accidents, vary. For instance, the cheerfulness and light manifested on a cloudless summer-day at noon, is very perceptibly more bright than that—than the light, that is—which feebly glimmers towards the close of a tempestuous wintry one. And again: the light which is shed, so to speak, full upon a sunny hill, appears greatly to surpass that which gleams into a deep ravine. And just in the same manner, there is a great and very perceptible difference observable in the enjoyment of the pleasantness and peace which are the essential characteristics of orthodox Church of England Christianity, according as the believer's spiritual state, the character of his faith, his former course of life, or other circumstances or accidents, vary. For instance, the pleasantness and peace enjoyed in the paths of the Christian religion by a believer, who, having been brought up in the nurture and admonition of the Lord from infancy, and attained unto a lively faith without having forsaken his own mercy so far as to constitute himself an enemy in his mind by wicked works, has afterwards proceeded from strength to strength, until he has become established unblameable in holiness, will incalculably exceed that experienced by one who, after having given himself over to work all iniquity with greediness, has been converted from the error of his ways, and attained unto faith, at the eleventh hour of his day of grace —will exceed it as observably and as incalculably as the light manifested on a cloudless summer-day at noon does that which glimmers towards the close of a lowering wintry one. And so, again; the believer who has attained unto a strong and stedfast faith, will enjoy a degree of pleasantness and peace which transcends that experienced by one whose faith is but weak and unstable, as obviously as the light shed full upon a sunny hill, does that which gleams into a deep ravine.

It follows, then, that in order to behold that pleasantness and peace which will be essential characteristics of Christianity, if the doctrine holden by the orthodox system of the Church of England with respect to the *origo originata* of justification be true, in the glory, if we may so speak, of their full manifestation, we must contemplate, as it were, the life of a Christian who has attained unto a lively faith of a strong and stedfast character, without having forsaken his own mercy, and who, continuing to walk according to this beginning, has proceeded from strength to strength until he has become established unblameable in holiness, or attained (in other words) to a full maturity in the Christian life; and that, at a time when (as is habitually, though not invariably, the case with such an one) he is in the unclouded enjoyment of that abundance of peace which is the covenanted inheritance of the righteous. Just as, if we wish to behold that cheerfulness and light which are essential characteristics of the day in the glory of their full manifestation, we must repair, at noon tide, to some sunny spot, on a cloudless summer's day. It follows also, that the fact of a high degree of pleasantness and peace not being experienced by every sincere believer in the paths of Christian godliness, affords no better ground for maintaining that pleasantness and peace are not essential characteristics of Christianity, than the fact that the dark places of the earth are not fully illumined, nor a lowering winter's evening made brilliant, by its radiance, does for contending that cheerfulness and light are not essential characteristics of the day. Moreover, it follows, that as the light of day, however feebly manifested, however intercepted by clouds and vapours, or otherwise divested of its full effulgence, possesses a character and properties peculiar to itself, and is essentially different from and superior to that proceeding from, or rather reflected by, any other luminary than the sun, or springing from any other source: so, that peace which will be an essential characteristic of Christianity if the doctrine holden by the orthodox system of the Church of England, with respect to the *origo originata* of justification, be true, however it may be broken in upon and deprived of the fulness of its blessedness, (as is the case when the believer has given himself over to work all iniquity with greediness in the past time of his life, and is, in consequence, corrected for his wickedness by an afflictive compunction) it will, notwithstanding, possess a character and properties, if we may so speak, peculiar to itself—it will be a peace which passeth all understanding—a peace which the world, or anything in the world, can neither give nor take away.

We would observe, in the second place; that, as, if the doctrine which we have shewn to be that holden by the orthodox system of the Church of England with respect to the *origo originata* of justification, be true, Christianity will possess a character analogous to that of the cheerfulness and light of day: so, if the doctrine taught by the system of the Authors of the Oxford Tracts, with respect to the *origo originata* of justification, were true and were believed, the character which Christianity would possess might be aptly described by that phrase of most mysterious and awful import, "the blackness of darkness."

That the Christianity, if we may so speak, of the system of the Authors of the Oxford Tracts does not possess a character so utterly repulsive and inimical to all peace and joy, that it might justly be described as "the blacknese of darkness," we admit. The cause, we conceive, why it does not possess such a character, is simply this.

Whilst Mr. Newman, and those who agree with him in maintaining the doctrine ' that the fulfilment of the law by a man's own doings, performed through a power conferred by the grace communicated at baptism, is the means appointed for the appropriation of a saving interest in our Redeemer's atonement to the individual,' distinctly repudiate and profess to renounce the doctrine, ' that faith is the means appointed for the appropriation of a saving interest in our Redeemer's atonement to the individual,' they virtually recognise, they partially hold it. They unconsciously admit it into their system (if we may so speak) to an extent which has the effect of modifying the doctrine they profess, so far as to prevent it from investing their system of religion with the character of " the blackness of darkness."

That Mr. Newman does virtually recognise and partially hold, at the same time that he openly repudiates and professes to renounce, the doctrine ' that faith is the means appointed for the appropriation of a saving interest in our Redeemer's atonement to the individual,'* is evident from the following passage, which contains, or constitutes rather, a summary of what he has said in an appendix to his lectures, entitled, " On the formal cause of Justification;"—viz.: " In this I conceive to lie the unity of Catholic doctrine on the subject of justification, that we are saved by Christ's imputed righteousness, and by our own inchoate righteousness at once;" ' that we are saved,' that is, 'partly by Christ's imputed righteousness, and partly by our own inchoate righteousness.'

Now, inasmuch as it is universally agreed that Christ's righteousness is upon, or imputed to, those that believe, and those that believe only, and is as it were a divinely appointed consequent of faith, it will follow that the doctrine that we are saved ' at once,' or ' partly ' by faith, and by our own inchoate righteousness, is precisely equivalent to, is the same doctrine expressed in other words, as the doctrine that we are saved " at once," or ' partly,' " by Christ's imputed righteousness, and by our own inchoate righteousness."

Consequently it is evident, from Mr. Newman's having made the statement which we have cited, that he must virtually recognise, and that he partially holds, the doctrine that ' we are saved by faith,' or ' that faith,' in other words, ' is the means appointed for the appropriation of a saving interest in our Redeemer's atonement to the individual,' at the same time that he openly repudiates, and professes to renounce, it.

It is plain, therefore, that when Mr. Newman and those who agree with him repudiate and profess to renounce the doctrine ' that faith is the means appointed for the appropriation of a saving interest in our Redeemer's atonement to the

---

* Vide Newman on Justification, p. 414.

individual, and constitutes the *origo originata*, or formal cause of justifiction,' at the same time that they virtually recognise and partially hold it, they act like certain persons adverted to by a late eminent divine,* who conceiving that they could dispense with, and professing to renounce, all benefit from the light of the sun, betook themselves to work by moonshine.

But be it observed, that although from the circumstance adverted to—because at the same time that they repudiate and profess to renounce the doctrine ' that faith is the means appointed for the appropriation of a saving interest in our Redeemer's atonement to the individual ;' Mr. Newman, and those who agree with him, virtually recognise and virtually hold it, the religion of their system does not possess a character so utterly repulsive and inimical to all peace and joy that it could justly be described as analogous to " the blackness of darkness :" yet notwithstanding that such is the case—notwithstanding that the doctrine holden by Mr. Newman and those who agree with him, when they so repudiate and profess to renounce the doctrine ' that faith is the means appointed for the appropriation of a saving interest in our Redeemer's atonement to the individual,' at the same time that they virtually recognise and partially hold it, has not the effect of investing the religion of their system with a character which can be justly described as analogous to " the blackness of darkness ;" it has the effect of investing it with a character, which, it is evident from what has been adduced in the course of the chapter to which these observations refer and the preceding appendices, is so far repulsive and inimical to all peace and joy, as to be justly describable as analogous to the darkness or rather feebly-illumined gloom of night.

And the light and cheerfulness of day does not differ more perceptibly and essentially from the darkness and gloom of night, than the character with which Christianity will be invested, if the doctrine taught by the orthodox system of the Church of England with respect to the *origo originata* of justification be true and be believed, does from that which it will possess if the doc-

---

* Bishop Middleton. We cite the observation from memory.

trine unavowedly, and unconsciously, but virtually, and as it were substantially holden by the system of the Authors of the Oxford Tracts, with respect to the *origo originata*, be true and be believed.

It will afford, as we imagine, not an additional proof—for that we hold to be needless—but a useful practical exemplification of the truth of what we have adduced above, if we supply a specimen, as it were, of the difference of character which Christianity will exhibit according as the doctrine taught by the orthodox system of the Church of England, or that holden by the system of the Authors of the Oxford Tracts, with respect to the *origo originata* of justification, is believed, by selecting a few extracts from certain documents and memoranda which put us in possession of the innermost feelings and secret affections, if we may so speak, and habits of thought of two individuals, one of whom believed the former and the other the latter, in such a manner as to enable us to discern the character of their religion with the most perfect distinctness.

The late Bishop Heber, as all who are in any degree conversant with his writings must be well aware, was a firm and conscientious believer in the doctrine which we have shewn to be that holden by the Church of England with respect to the *origo originata* of justification.

In his private journal and letters he thus expresses himself:

" The blessings of this life may become a source of religious comfort. From the reflection that they are all God's gifts, every enjoyment will receive a higher colouring, and the more happy we are, the more earnestly we shall long for an admission to that heaven where we shall see the hand that blesses us, and really experience what we now know but faintly, how pleasant it is to be thankful. There have been moments, I am ashamed to say how seldom, when my heart has burst within me with the conviction which I have just described."

" I am in truth a prosperous man, who has unremitting causes of gratitude, and whose principal apprehension it ought to be that he has a greater share of earthly happiness than he knows how to manage."

" I fully believe, and it is a belief without which I could not be happy, 'that the sorrows to which in different ways we all must be liable, are as truly designed for our improvement and advantage as the physic which we give to a sick man."

"Although every Christian should be prepared to meet obloquy in the cause of his Master, since it is a visitation which happens to many, and may happen to all, yet it is not universally or necessarily brought on us by the strictest piety."

"The experiment" (that of the administration of the Lord's Supper on board the East Indiaman in which his voyage to India was performed) "has been most satisfactory; and I ought to be, and I hope am, very grateful for the opportunities of doing good which seem to be held out to me."

"Learn to trust God more entirely and hopefully; trust that his love for you in Jesus Christ, will do more, far more for you than you can for yourself; and that if you cast your cares on Him He will care for you. I have been long aware that in the honest humbleness of your heart, you have thought more painfully of your own condition, than one who cherishes a firm faith on the Rock of ages, and an ardent desire after holiness need do. Remember who He is in whom you have hoped. Be sure that both body and soul are safe under His protection so long as we wait patiently on him, and resist the temptations against which we are compelled to struggle: and, believe me, that while this hope continues to increase in you, both body and soul will derive a daily increase of strength and cheerfulness."

The late Rev. Richard Hurrell Froude was a contributor to, and one we believe of the principal authors of, the system of the Oxford Tracts.*

In his private journal he expresses himself as follows:—

"I have been coming to a resolution that, as soon as I am out of the reach of observation, I will begin a sort of monastic austere life, and do my best to chastise myself before the Lord."

"Oct. 24.—I have been put out this evening, by hearing

---

* The publication of the "Remains of the late Rev. H. Froude, from which the following extracts are taken, was designed to support the views of the Authors of the Oxford Tracts; as we learn from the preface; vide Preface, p. xvii.

that I am not to receive any thing for my fellowship till this time next year. I ought to acquiesce in it with complete indifference, but it will cut me off for a time from exercises of virtue, which I intended to have begun with directly. However I can make it up by other additional austerity and self-denial, in order to compensate for not giving alms."

"Oct. 27.—I forgot to mention that I had been looking round my rooms, and thinking they looked comfortable and nice, and that I said in my heart, 'Ah, ah! I am warm;' and felt less anxious to find an opportunity of giving them up to Mr. ———, which, however, I am resolved to do. It is disgusting for a fellow, like me, to be enjoying the fat of the land. I was not up till half-past six; slept on the floor, and a nice uncomfortable time I had of it."

"Nov. 10.—Fell quite short of my wishes, with respect to the rigour of to-day's fast, though I am quite willing to believe not unpardonably: I tasted nothing till after half-past eight in the evening, and before that had undergone more uncomfortableness, both of body and mind, than any fast has as yet occasioned me."

"Nov. 12.—Felt great reluctance to sleep on the floor last night, and was nearly arguing myself out of it."

"Nov. 16.—I am weary of finishing the course I have prescribed to myself: the enthusiasm which set me off has gradually died away, and I am left to go on resolutions, the aim of which I often lose sight of, in spite of discouragements, for which I had hardly prepared myself."

"I am convinced acts of benevolence and humility are the only pleasures of earthly existence."

"Dec. 4.—I awoke at three in the night......The enthusiastic misery of yesterday is enough to warn me that I was not right."

We leave the two series of extracts, which have been given, to speak for themselves.

They will do so far more effectually than any commentary framed out of the multitude of thoughts which suggest themselves on a perusal of them could possibly have done!

CHAPTER V.

In the preceding pages, we have adduced three several cases in which a variance is observable betwixt the errors holden by Socinianism and the Protestantism spoken of by the Authors of the Oxford Tracts; and have shewn that in each case, the course taken by the system of the Authors of the Oxford Tracts is irreconcileably different from that holden by the orthodox system of the Church of England.

Now, upon principle, it stands to reason, that of these several different courses so taken by the system of the Authors of the Oxford Tracts and the orthodox system of the Church of England, in the cases adverted to, those taken by the former must of necessity diverge nearer to Popery than those taken by the latter. For the system of the Authors of the Oxford Tracts, being constituted (as we have seen that it is) upon the principle of holding the *via media,* or preserving a mean, as nearly as possible, between the Protestantism spoken of (a way—or which is as a point, let us say, for the sake of precision in our argument,—situate within the extreme error or ulterior point of Socinianism, from which the orthodox system of the Church of England computes its admeasurement of the *via media* which it takes) and Popery (the way or point from which both systems calculate the *via media* which they take in common), it may be demonstrated with mathematical certainty that the several courses which it takes, in the cases adverted to, when holding the *via media* between Popery and Protestantism spoken of, must of necessity diverge nearer towards Popery than the several courses taken, in the cases adverted to, by the orthodox system of the Church of England, when holding the *via media* between Popery and that extreme error or ulterior point which the Protestantism spoken of is within.

But it may, notwithstanding, be of advantage—it will tend (as we trust) to convince our readers more palpably of the danger attendant upon an unadvised adoption of their opinions, if we point out specifically how and to what extent the course taken, or doctrine taught, by the system of the Authors of the Oxford Tracts in the several cases adverted to, diverges towards the errors holden by the Romanists upon the points which they respectively involve: we propose, therefore, to subjoin a few observations with a view of doing so.

With regard, then, to the first of the three cases adverted to: viz., as to the course holden by the system of the Authors of the Oxford Tracts, with respect to 'authority.'

We have seen that the error holden by the Romanists, with respect to 'authority'—with respect to that supreme and uncontrolled or paramount power of adjudication upon doubtful or disputed points, of which it is in the nature of things impossible that two can co-exist, is this:

'That an infallible authority has been committed to their church.'

'That "authority" resides in Catholic or primitive tradition:'

Is (as we have seen) the doctrine holden by the system of the Authors of the Oxford Tracts, with respect to the point in question.

Now it stands to reason, that if there be an authority such as that of which we speak in Catholic tradition, any decision or opinion pronounced in the exercise of that authority must be implicitly deferred to. For were this not the case; if a man were at liberty to defer to, or reject, any such decision or opinion, according as he judged it to be right or wrong, the authority of Catholic tradition would be nominal only. It would be idle, in that case, to say that authority, or a supreme and uncontrolled power of adjudication, with respect to doubtful or disputed points, resided in Catholic tradition. It is evident, therefore, that those who maintain 'that authority resides in Catholic tradition,' must of necessity hold that any decision or adjudication pronounced in the exercise of that authority must be implicitly deferred to. And that being the case, it follows, that if the authority of which we speak resides in Catholic tradition, that authority must virtually be invested with the character of infallibility. We may call it 'indefectibility,' if we will, instead of 'infallibility,' as is done by the Authors of the Oxford Tracts; but this change of denomination will not in any respect alter the essential nature of the character or attribute itself.

When a man has come to the conclusion, that an infallible or indefectible authority resides in Catholic tradition; and (as such an one must necessarily do) considers it to be incumbent upon him to go (as Bishop Jebb terms it) to Catholic tradition for an adjudication upon any doubtful or disputed point, and to defer implicitly to any such adjudication when ascertained or pronounced, it must of course become a matter of most serious inquiry with him, ' as to how such adjudication of Catholic tradition is to be obtained.' And this inquiry it is evident will be inseparably connected with, indeed, may be said to resolve itself into, another more general or leading one: viz., 'As to what constitutes Catholic tradition.'

Now it is clear that 'what constitutes Catholic tradition,' and 'how its adjudication is to be obtained,' can be determined only by one or other of the two following methods: viz., by an exercise of the private judgment of each individual; or by some fiat, or authoritative award, independent of private judgment.

Supposing that we hold that the questions, as to

'what constitutes Catholic tradition,' and as to 'how the adjudication of Catholic tradition is to be obtained,' are to be determined by an exercise of private judgment; and maintain, as we must do in that case, that if a man wish for an adjudication upon any doubtful or disputed point, he must go to Catholic tradition, he himself determining, by an exercise of his private judgment, what it is that constitutes Catholic tradition; we invest private judgment with what may be very intelligibly designated as an appellant jurisdiction or paramount authority over Catholic tradition.

For, in the case supposed, one man, in the exercise of his private judgment, may pronounce that the ordinances of the first six œcumenical councils constitute Catholic tradition; and another man determine, in a like exercise of his private judgment, that the ordinances of other councils than, or of not so many as, the first six œcumenical councils constitute Catholic tradition; and the adjudication obtained upon a reference to it, may differ, and possibly be contrariant, according as the one or other of the above mentioned decisions of private judgment, as to what constitutes Catholic tradition, may be adopted and deferred to.

It is evident, therefore, that it is to some fiat or authoritative award, independent of private judgment, that those who hold 'that authority resides in Catholic tradition,' must look for a decision as to what constitutes Catholic tradition.

Now let us suppose that an ingenuous individual

who was convinced that an infallible, or indefectible authority resided in Catholic tradition, and had satisfied himself that it was to some fiat or authoritative award, independent of private judgment, that he must look for a decision as to 'what constituted Catholic tradition,' and as to 'how its adjudication was to be obtained;' and who proceeded, in consequence, to inquire 'where?' or 'in what?' the power of pronouncing any such fiat or authoritative award had been appointed to reside; happened to enter into disputation upon the subject with a zealous and tolerably well-informed Roman-catholic. The Roman-catholic would, unhesitatingly, assert 'that the power of pronouncing a fiat or authoritative award, as to 'what constituted Catholic tradition,' and ' how its adjudication was to be obtained,' had been ' committed to his church;' and contend ' that, admitting, as the inquirer did, ' that a power of pronouncing a fiat or authoritative award, independent of private judgment, as to what constituted Catholic tradition, must of necessity be lodged somewhere,' he could not point out—there did not exist (the Roman Catholic would urge) any depository (so to speak) of the power of pronouncing such fiat or authoritative award which had a better claim to be such depository than that advanced by the Roman-catholic church; or any to which the power of pronouncing such fiat or authoritative award could (all things considered) be more fitly and reasonably committed.' And when he did so—when the Roman-catholic disputant asserted this—what could the inquirer of whom we speak reply? If, as we have supposed, he were one too ingenuous to deceive himself, and delude others by a recourse to any ingenious but fallacious subtilties, he would find himself constrained to admit that he could not point out any. And the consequence would be, that the inquirer of whom we speak would be under the necessity of either taking one step forward, as it were, into Popery, or retiring from the position, if we may so speak, to which he had advanced, by renouncing the doctrine, ' that ' authority' resides in Catholic tradition.'

It is evident, therefore, that the course taken by the system of the Authors of the Oxford Tracts, with respect to ' authority,' may be said to approach to the very verge of Popery.

' That Holy Orders is a sacrament '—is a sacrament, that is, in the recognized and legitimate sense of the word: viz., an outward and visible sign, whereby an inward and spiritual grace is conferred upon the individual ordained—is the doctrine holden by the Romanists, with respect to the second of the cases adverted to.

' That Ordination is a rite which confers a special description and degree of personal grace upon the individual ordained '—is that taught by the system of the Authors of the Oxford Tracts.

CHAPTER V. 97

Now we have seen * that the objectionable character of the doctrine holden by the Romanists, when they maintain that ' Holy Orders as a sacrament, consists in the tendency which it has to generate an inordinate and superstitious veneration for the priesthood: that being the natural and inevitable effect of that belief, ' that the priest is endowed with a superiority of spiritual being,' which is a necessary consequence of holding that ordination sacramentally confers an inward and spiritual or personal grace upon the priest.

Now it is evident that the doctrine taught by the system of the Authors of the Oxford Tracts, ' that ordination is a rite which confers a special description and degree of personal grace upon the individual ordained,' will also have the effect of superinducing a belief, ' that the priest is endued with a superiority of spiritual being.'

For the priest (in the case supposed) being endued, at ordination, with a certain description and degree of inward and spiritual or personal grace, of which he is the exclusive participant, over and above that which he receives in common with the layman, by virtue of the sacraments of Baptism and the Lord's Supper, and the other means of grace accessible to both, must, it is evident, possess means which (if duly improved) will enable him to attain

---

* Vide. p. 36.

CHAPTER V.

to a higher elevation of spiritual character than the unordained layman, who is not made a partaker of such additional grace, can by any possibility arrive at. And if he thus possess the germ, if we may so speak, of a higher elevation of spiritual character, the priest may be said to be 'endued with a superiority of spiritual being;' for the two propositions are convertible. And this belief, 'that the priest is endowed with a superiority of spiritual being,' will, of course, have the same tendency in the one case, as it has in the other—that of generating an inordinate and superstitious veneration for the priesthood.*

It follows, therefore, that with respect to the second of the three cases adduced, the doctrine taught by the system of the authors of the Oxford Tracts will possess the same objectionable character as that holden by the Romanists upon the point which it involves. Nay, it is evident that the two doctrines are virtually identical, and differ but in the terms in which they are propounded.

Before we proceed to point out how, in the third of the three cases adverted to, the course taken, or doctrine taught, by the system of the Authors of the Oxford Tracts, diverges towards Popery, we are under the necessity of introducing a brief statement of the doctrine holden by the Roman-catholic church, with respect to the *origo originata* of justification.

---

* Vide Justificative Appendix to Chapter V.

'The groundwork, if we may so speak, of the doctrine holden by the Romanists, with respect to the *origo originata* of justification, may be stated to be that in which it is made to consist by Mr. Newman: viz., ' that justification consists in renewal of the Holy Ghost.'

If, after his justification, through that ' renewal of the Holy Ghost,' which the sacrament of baptism communicates, the Christian do not commit deadly sin, he retains this justification; but inasmuch as the sins of infirmity, of which all men commit more or less, will have impaired the justification which the Christain obtained at baptism, to a certain degree, and thereby rendered him unmeet for the presence of that God who is of purer eyes than to behold iniquity, extreme unction, another sacrament (according to the Roman-catholic doctrine) or rite attended with an especial Divine efficacy and ministering (so to speak) renewal of the Holy Ghost, administered when he is *in extremis*, and no longer able to commit sin, is holden to be necessary, in order to re-integrate the Christian's impaired justification.

But if, after his justification, through that renewal of the Holy Ghost, which the sacrament of baptism communicates, the Christian commit deadly sin, he loses, forfeits this justification (according to the Roman-catholic doctrine) and the renewal of the Holy Ghost communicated at baptism; and continues in an unjustified state, until justification, by a like renewal of the Holy Ghost, is re-communicated to him by another sacrament or rite attended with an especial Divine efficacy and ministering renewal of the Holy Ghost: viz., the sacrament of penance.

Moreover, after the justification and renewal of the Holy Ghost communicated to him by the sacrament of baptism or penance, a man may commit wilful sins of a venial character (sins, that is, which do not occasion the forfeiture of his justification) which he neglects to confess, and which therefore remain punishable; or he may commit deadly sins of so aggravated a character that, notwithstanding he should repent of them, and be restored to a state of justification and renewal by the sacrament of penance, they expose him to ' vindictive chastisement,' as it is termed. And the sins so committed (in common with various other offences, we believe) must be expiated, according to the Roman-catholic doctrine, in purgatory,—a place of torment into which those who die in what may be termed an imperfect state of justification, descend and are detained,

> " 'Till the foul crimes done in [their] days of nature
> Are burnt and purged away."

The above statement of what (as we conceive) is the doctrine taught by the Roman-catholic church, with respect to the *origo originata* of justification, will be sufficient for our purpose. We will offer but one remark with reference to it: viz., that it is evident that the Roman-catholic tenets which inculcate the necessity of the sacraments of penance and extreme unction, and the existence of purgatory, are inseparably connected with and dependent, as it were, upon the doctrine, that 'justification consists in renewal of the Holy Ghost.' In truth, it is, properly speaking, all the tenets to which we have had occasion to advert above, taken together, that constitute the doctrine taught by the Roman-catholic church, with respect to the *origo originata* of justification.

'That justification consists in a renewal of the Holy Ghost, communicated at baptism, completed by the fulfilment of the law by a man's own doings,'* is the doctrine taught by the system of the authors of the Oxford Tracts, with respect to the *origo originata* of justification.

Now let us suppose that an ingenuous individual, who has adopted Mr. Newman's views upon the subject of justification, and become a convert to the system of the Authors of the Oxford Tracts; and who, in consequence, maintains the doctrine, 'that justification consists in a renewal of the Holy Ghost, communicated at baptism, completed by the fulfilment of the law, by a man's own doings;' should chance to meet with a zealous and tolerably well-

---

* It is obvious that the above doctrine is the same in substance as the doctrine, 'that the fulfilment of the law, by a man's own doings, performed through a power conferred by the grace communicated at baptism, is the means appointed for the appropriation of a saving interest in our Redeemer's atonement to the individual.'

informed Roman-catholic, and were to enter into disputation with him as to the *origo originata* of justification.

'According to, or rather consistently with, the doctrine of our church' (the Roman-catholic might affirm), ' if a man were to preserve the justification, through renewal of the Holy Ghost communicated to him at baptism, wholly unimpaired by leading a perfectly sinless life, (by fulfilling the law of God, that, is in all things), he would, at his decease, be perfectly justified, and meet for the inheritance of the saints in light, without being under the necessity of resorting to any additional sacrament or instrument of justification. Now it is evident (the Roman-catholic might proceed) that this doctrine of ours is exactly tantamount to, is virtually the same as, your doctrine, ' that justification consists in a renewal of the Holy Ghost, communicated at baptism, completed by the fulfilment of the law by a man's own doings.' The only difference between the two is, the simple verbal one, occasioned by your saying that the fulfilment of the law ' completes,' whilst we say that the fulfilment of the law ' preserves unimpaired,' that justification by renewal of the Holy Ghost, communicated at baptism.

'We agree thus far in our views with respect to the *origo originata* of justification:' the Roman-catholic disputant might continue. 'Where we differ is here: we maintain that no man can perfectly fulfil the law of God; but that the holiest of men commit numberless sins of infirmity; which sins of infirmity, we contend, have the effect of impairing that justification which the Christian obtained at baptism, and rendering it so far incomplete, that another sacrament or rite attended with an especial Divine efficacy and ministering (so to speak) an additional renewal of the Holy Ghost, is necessary to re-integrate such impaired justification. And we hold, in consequence, that extreme unction is necessary. Whereas, whilst you admit (as your church declares) that man is very far gone from original righteousness, and that an " infection of nature " has been permitted to remain in the baptized, notwithstanding that renewal of the Holy Ghost which baptism communicates; you at the same time, maintain ' that justification consists in a renewal of the Holy Ghost communicated at baptism, completed by a fulfilment of the law.' It is self-evident therefore, that, according to your view of the doctrine of justification, it is absolutely impossible that any man can die justified, inasmuch as it is not possible for any man to fulfil the law.

The conclusion which the Roman-catholic disputant would deduce, and fairly deduce, from his premises, would be this:—that since the disciple of Mr. Newman, and convert to the system of the Authors of the Oxford Tracts, agreed with him in holding ' that justification consists in a renewal of the Holy Ghost, which can only be ' preserved unimpaired,' or (as is precisely the same thing) ' completed' by the fulfilment of the law;' and also agreed with him in admitting, 'that man is very far gone from original righteousness, and subject to an "infection of nature," notwithstanding such renewal of the Holy Ghost communicated at baptism, and cannot therefore fulfil the law.' We must needs agree with him in maintaining, 'that some other sacrament or rite attended with an especial Divine efficacy and ministering an additional renewal of the Holy Ghost, is necessary to re-integrate the Christian's impaired, or, as the same thing, to complete his imperfect, justification;' and, in consequence, admit that the sacrament of extreme unction is necessary, and acknowledge that the Roman-catholic doctrine, which teaches its necessity, is right.

To this the disciple of Mr. Newman, and convert to the system of the Authors of the Oxford Tracts, would probably reply: 'We consider that no such sacrament is necessary, because, if a man fulfil the law as well as he is able, after having done all in his power to slaughter and cast out the sin of his nature, the deficiency in his obedience is supplied, and his imperfect justification completed, by the imputation of Christ's righteousness.

Now we will suppose that the Roman-catholic disputant waived the rejoinder that he might very reasonably have made, 'that the doctrine last stated by his opponent was a very different one from that which he had originally maintained;' and also all question as to 'whether the doctrine that Christ's righteousness is imputed to men to make up for a deficiency in their own doings, were not an heterodox one;' and proceeded to observe:

'That he (the Roman-catholic disputant), and the disciple of Mr. Newman, and convert to the system of the Authors of the Oxford Tracts, were entirely of accord upon another point: inasmuch as both maintain 'that, if after the justification and renewal of the Holy Ghost communicated at baptism, a man commit sin of a certain aggravated character, he forfeits such justification and renewal.'*

'When a man has thus lost the justification and renewal of the Holy Ghost communicated by the sacrament of baptism, they must be recommunicated, as we hold, (the Roman-catholic might continue) by another sacrament or rite attended with an especial divine efficacy and ministering renewal of the Holy Ghost; viz., the sacrament of penance. And since you agree with us in maintaining 'that by committing sin of a certain aggravated description, a man loses the justification and renewal communicated by the sacrament of baptism; you must also agree with us in holding 'that they must be re-communicated to him by some other sacrament or rite attended with an especial divine efficacy and ministering renewal of the Holy Ghost:' or it will follow, 'that when a man has once lost the justification and renewal communicated at baptism, as you admit that he may do,

---

* Vide Newman on Justification, pp. 169, 170, 171.

it will no longer be possible for him to be justified,' supposing that 'justification consists in renewal of the Holy Ghost, completed by the fulfilment of the law by a man's own doings,' as you assert that it does.* 'In this case (the Roman-catholic might justly observe) it will be in vain for you to allege 'that the imputation of Christ's righteousness would avail to such an one's justification;' for not to mention that by maintaining this you manifestly make Christ the minister of sin, you cannot assert it, (it is evident), without repudiating the doctrine ' that justification consists in renewal of the Holy Ghost, completed by the fulfilment of the law by a man's own doings.' It follows therefore that agreeing with us in maintaining 'that by committing sin of a certain aggravated description, a man loses the justification and renewal communicated at baptism,' you must also agree with us in holding 'that they must be recommunicated to him by some other sacrament ;' and agreeing with us in this, you must admit that our sacrament of penance is a necessary one, and that the doctrine which inculcates its necessity is right.'

This, we conceive, the disciple of Mr. Newman, and convert to the system of the Oxford Tracts, would be under the necessity of granting.

Upon resuming his conference with the disciple of Mr. Newman, and convert to the system of the Au-

---

* Vide Appendix, No. 2.

thors of the Oxford Tracts, the Roman-catholic disputant might proceed:

'We agree, as I have shewn, in maintaining that 'justification consists in a renewal of the Holy Ghost communicated at baptism,' 'completed' (according to your view) 'by the fulfilment of the law, or by obedience, perfected as to its incompleteness through human infirmity, by the imputation of Christ's righteousness,' or 'retained' (according to our view) 'by a holy life, and perfected, as respects the incompleteness of its retention, through the commission of sins of infirmity, by the sacrament of extreme unction;' and also in holding ' that if, after his justification and renewal by the Holy Ghost, a man commit sin of a certain aggravated character, he forfeits such justification and renewal. We concur, moreover, upon another point of very material importance. For we (the Roman-catholics) maintain that if, after justification and renewal of the Holy Ghost, a man commit sins which we denominate venial, as opposed to deadly, which he neglects to confess, he impairs his justification to a degree proportionate to the number and magnitude of his transgressions, but does not wholly forfeit it: and you maintain what is in effect precisely the same doctrine when you teach that " when a man declines in obedience he diminishes his justification,"* to a degree, of course, pro-

---

* Vide Newman on Justification, p. 169.

portionate to the extent of such declension, but does not wholly lose it.

Now, since you agree with us upon this point, you must either go further and agree with us when we maintain 'that where a man dies in such an impaired or diminished state of justification, he has to expiate the sins which have impaired or diminished his justification, in a place of punishment to which his spirit is consigned in the intermediate state;' or hold that one who dies in such an impaired or diminished state of justification, will be consigned to eternal perdition, notwithstanding that he dies partially justified; which it would be absurd for you to do.

'Again;' (the Roman-catholic disputant might proceed), 'you agree with us, as was before observed, in holding that if, after justification and renewal of the Holy Ghost, a man commit sin of a certain aggravated character, he forfeits such justification and renewal.'

'Now supposing that a baptized Christian has committed sin of this aggravated character—has given himself over, let us say, to work all iniquity with greediness,' and has lost in consequence the justification and renewal which he had obtained at baptism; but is afterwards restored to a state of justification and renewal by the sacrament of penance or (for the sake of argument, we will say) by any other means, and dies shortly, or immediately, let us say, after he has been so restored.

In this case, if you hold that such an one—one who has not made the slightest progress in obedience, or fulfilled a tittle of the law,—will die perfectly justified, and meet for the inheritance of the saints in light, either in consequence of the imputation of Christ's righteousness or otherwise howsoever, you disavow— you directly contradict and impugn that doctrine, or branch of the doctrine, of justification for which you especially contend, and which constitutes, as you affirm, the specific difference between your views upon the subject and our own.* Neither can you hold that one who died partially justified, would be consigned to eternal perdition. Consequently your only alternative is that of holding with us, 'that one, who, after having given himself over to work all iniquity with greediness, instead of making any progress in the fulfilment of the law, is restored to his forfeited justification and renewal of the Holy Ghost, and dies immediately, or shortly afterwards, must expiate his sins, or have that sin of his nature (which, according to your doctrine, should have been slaughtered and cast out by obedience †) slaughtered and cast out in a place of punishment to which his spirit is consigned in the intermediate state.' And if you agree with us in holding 'that one who dies in an imperfect state of justification, and one who has given himself

---

* Vide p. 51, and the passages in Newman on Justification there referred to.
† Vide Newman on Justification, pe. 205.

over to work all iniquity with greediness, before he received the re-communication of justification and the renewal of the Holy Ghost, after receiving which he presently died, must expiate his sins in a place of punishment to which his spirit is consigned in the intermediate state;' you must necessarily admit that our doctrine which teaches the existence of purgatory is right—is substantially sound and true.*

The two following conclusions are (as we trust) indisputably established by the preceding observations :—

First, that the doctrine holden by the Authors of the system of the Oxford Tracts with respect to the *origo originata* of justification—the doctrine 'that justification consists in renewal of the Holy Ghost, completed by the fulfilment of the law,' is in the main and in its principle identical with the doctrine taught by the Roman-catholic Church with respect to the *origo originata* of justification, which (when propounded in general terms) may be correctly stated to be this, 'that justification consists in renewal of the Holy Ghost, retained unimpaired by the fulfilment of the law.'

Secondly, that since the Authors of the Oxford Tracts hold a doctrine with respect to the *origo originata* of justification which is the same in the main and in its principle with that taught by the

---

* Vide Appendix to No. 3.

Roman-catholic Church, they must of necessity also hold certain tenets which are necessary and inseparable adjuncts, which constitute, if we may so speak, an essential part and parcel of the Roman-catholic doctrine of justification; and must therefore hold tenets which are the same as, or answerable to, the Roman-catholic tenets, which teach the necessity of the sacraments of penance and extreme unction, and the existence of purgatory; which are such necessary and inseparable adjuncts to the doctrine 'that justification consists in renewal of the Holy Ghost, completed, or retained unimpaired, by the fulfilment of the law,' if it be admitted (as it is) that "an infection of nature" has been permitted to remain in man, notwithstanding his renewal by the Holy Ghost.

We would observe, in conclusion, that in the course of the preceding remarks we have (as we trust) indisputably shewn, that the course holden, or doctrine taught, by the system of the Authors of the Oxford Tracts, in the first of the three cases which have been adduced, approaches to the very verge of Popery; and is of such a character (if we may so speak) that he who holds it cannot maintain his ground, when duly pressed, but will be under the necessity of advancing within the confines of Popery, or of retiring from the position he has occupied; and that in the second and third of the three cases adduced, the courses taken or doctrines taught by the system of the Authors of the Oxford Tracts, are virtually identical with, and as erroneous and exceptionable as, the courses taken or doctrines taught by the Roman-catholic Church upon the points which they respectively involve.

JUSTIFICATIVE APPENDIX TO CHAP. V.

No. 1.

It may be advisable to remark, that the doctrine taught by the system of the Authors of the Oxford Tracts, with respect to ordination, will still possess a character which virtually identifies it with, and renders it equally objectionable as, the doctrine taught by the Romanists with respect to Holy Orders; notwithstanding it may be admitted 'that the description and degree of personal grace conferred upon the priest at ordination (according to the doctrine taught by the system of the Authors of the Oxford Tracts,) is so conferred as a trust from Christ for the benefit of His people.'

For granting, as we must do in the case supposed, that that higher elevation of spiritual character unattainable by the layman, at which the priest might arrive if he duly improved that exclusive personal grace (if we may so term it) conferred upon him at ordination, was intended to redound to the benefit of Christ's people, by enabling the priest to exhibit a brighter example of holiness for their imitation, or to teach and exhort with a greater moral authority and force, or otherwise howsoever; yet a belief 'that the priest was placed in a state in which he was exclusively capable of attaining to such higher elevation of spiritual character,' or (which is exactly tantamount) 'that the priest is endued with a superiority of spiritual being' for a particular purpose, (if we may so speak) will, it is evident, have the same effect as a belief that he was placed in a state in which he was exclusively capable of attaining to such higher elevation of spiritual character,' or 'was endued' (in other words) with a 'superiority of spiritual being' for a general one.'

It would equally lead, or have a tendency to lead, to an inordinate and superstitious veneration for the priesthood; and in consequence, superinduce, or at least be calculated to generate, the same, or similar and equally pernicious and objectionable errors as those Romish ones, which, as we before remarked, have their source in an inordinate and superstitious veneration for the priesthood.

No. 2.

It is scarcely necessary to observe that it is impossible to maintain, (as some of our readers may, possibly, feel disposed to do) that the sacrament of the Lord's Supper may be resorted to for the purpose of re communicating the justification and renewal spoken of in the text. For it is certain that one who partook of the Lord's Supper under the circumstances adverted to—when he had forfeited the justification and renewal communicated (according to the doctrine spoken of in the passage to which these observations refer) at baptism, by committing sin of an aggravated character, and was not therefore in a state of grace, must necessarily receive it unworthily.

As we have had occasion to allude to the sacrament of the Lord's Supper, it occurs to us to remark, before we quit the subject, that we do not assume (as the careless reader may, perhaps, be apt to suppose) that little or no efficacy is ascribed to it either by the Roman-catholics or the Authors of the system of the Oxford Tracts: but since, be the efficacy of the sacrament of the Lord's supper what it may (according to the two systems adverted to), it evidently is not so great as to have the effect of preserving the Christian's justification wholly unimpaired in the one case, or rendering his obedience perfect in the other; we have omitted any particular allusion to it in the compendia of doctrine which we have given, for the sake of conciseness and perspicuity.

No. 3.

It may perhaps occur to the reader to inquire, with some anxiety, 'how one who holds the doctrine taught by the orthodox system of the Church of England, with respect to the *origo originata* of justification, can reject the Roman-catholic doc- of purgatory consistently with a belief that one who has given himself over to work all iniquity with greediness in the past time of his life, can be saved if he die shortly or immediately after he has been converted from the error of his ways and attained unto a lively faith, and before he has time or opportunity to perform good works.'

For the satisfaction of any such inquirer, we would observe, that one who holds the doctrine taught by the orthodox system of the Church of England, with respect to the *origo originata* of justification—who believes ' that a lively faith attained unto through the grace communicated at baptism is the means divinely appointed for the appropriation of a saving interest in our Redeemer's atonement to the individual,' and who consistently, nay, in necessary connection (we may say) with this belief, holds, with an inspired Apostle, that the righteousness of Christ is upon, or imputed to, all that believe, and that, in consequence, "all that believe are justified from all things;"* can very consistently reject the Romish doctrine of purgatory, at the same time that he believes and maintains that a baptized Christian, who, after having forsaken his own mercy so far as to have given himself over to work all iniquity with greediness, attains unto a lively faith, and dies before he has time or opportunity to manifest that faith by a holy walk and conversation, will be saved, and meet at once for the inheritance of the saints in light.

It is true, indeed, that in the case supposed—when one who has led a notoriously profligate life professes to have been converted from the error of his ways, and to have attained unto a lively faith, and dies without having had time or opportunity to evince the sincerity of his faith by a holy walk and conversation, it will (for the most part) remain doubtful—not whether he were saved, supposing him to have attained unto a true and lively faith—but whether he had attained unto a true and lively laith, whether the faith professed and perhaps felt,

---

* Acts xxxix. 13.

as he conceived, by such an one, were of that true and lively character of which a loving heart to keep God's commandments is the inseparable concomitant.

But although this may be the case frequently, and perhaps for the most part; yet it is not invariably the case. For, happily, instances occasionally occur when little (if any) doubt can be entertained as to the true and saving character of the faith professed by one who, after having given himself over to work all iniquity with greediness in the past time of his life, attains to such professed faith on his death bed.

The case of the well known Earl of Rochester furnishes so remarkable a one, that we are induced to advert to it more particularly.

After having lived a life, which it would be impossible by the fullest and most laboured narration to describe more vividly than we may do by terming it, in the language of Scripture, the life of one who "had given himself over to work all uncleanness with greediness," John, the second Earl of Rochester, became the victim of a mortal disease, superinduced, there can be little doubt, by his criminal excesses. During the progress of this death-bed illness, which lasted about nine weeks, the Earl of Rochester attained to faith through the more immediate instrumentality (if we so speak) of a perusal of the fifty-third chapter of Isaiah, and comparison of its contents with the narrative of the life and death of our Saviour as recorded in the Gospels.

"He died a most exemplary penitent," says Bishop Burnet in the account which he has given of his "life and death." "Now he is at rest," continues the Bishop; "and, I am very confident, enjoys the fruits of his late, but sincere, repentance."

The state of the case (if we may so speak) with respect to the Earl of Rochester and other sincere penitents similarly situated, is (as it appears to us) simply this. The faith attained to is a lively faith, a faith of which a loving heart to keep God's commandments is the inseparable concomitant, although its sincerity be not manifested by the good works which it would assuredly have produced, had not the time and opportunity for their performance been providentially denied.

That the Earl of Rochester's faith was one of which a loving heart to keep God's commandments was the concomitant, appears to be indisputably evident from the account of his life and death before alluded to, and from that given in a funeral sermon preached by the clergyman who attended him in the absence of Bishop Burnet. " He wished," it is related in the latter, amongst many other expressions equally indicative of the " abhorrency " with which he reflected upon his former course of life, " that he had been a starving leper crawling in a ditch ; that he had been a link-boy or a beggar, or for his whole life confined to a dungeon, rather than to have sinned against God as e had done."

CHAPTER VI.

Now we have seen that the way or course taken by the system of the Authors of the Oxford Tracts, in accordance with its principle of holding the *via media*, or preserving a mean as nearly as possible between the Protestantism spoken of and Popery, will differ from that taken by the orthodox system of the Church of England, in accordance with its principle of holding the *via media*, or preserving a mean as nearly as possible between Popery and Socinianism, in the several cases which have been adduced, and upon every other point upon Socinianism and the Protestantism spoken of, are not of accord. And we have also seen, that when the ways or courses respectively taken, as above-mentioned, by the system of the Authors of the Oxford Tracts and the orthodox system of the Church of England, do so differ, the way or course taken by the former will diverge nearer to Popery than that taken by the latter. It follows, therefore, that the way or course so taken, as aforesaid, by the system of the Authors of the Oxford Tracts, may be said to be situate in a tract—we speak in language of a figurative character, because (as we conceive) we are thereby able to express our meaning more intelligibly—which lies between the *via media* holden by the orthodox system of the Church of England, and the way or course taken by Popery; assuming (as we will do, for the sake of argument) that the two courses taken by Popery, and the system of the Authors of the Oxford Tracts, do not become one and the same.

We have seen, moreover, that between the way or course which the orthodox system of the Church of England holds in accordance with its principle of taking the *via media*, or preserving a mean as nearly as possible, between Popery and Socinianism, and the extreme or cardinal error of Socinianism, there lies another tract within which divers ways are situate, and, amongst them, those respectively taken by the Protestantism spoken of by the Authors of the Oxford Tracts, and the Evangelical party in our Church.*

It is evident, then, that at the same time that it holds the *via media*, which we have seen that it takes between the extreme or cardinal errors of Popery and Socinianism, or between the ways (in other words) taken by Popery and Socinianism; the orthodox system of the Church of England also holds the *via media* between that way or course, situate in the tract lying between the *via media* that it takes and Socinianism, which is taken by the Protes-

---

* Vide Chapter I., and Appendices, Nos. 1 & 2.

tantism spoken of, and the Evangelical party in our Church, and that way or course, situate in the tract lying between the *via media* which it takes and Popery, which is taken by the system of the Authors of the Oxford Tracts; or (in other words) between the mean errors of the Evangelical and Apostolical systems.*

The annexed synopsis may serve (as we trust) to render our meaning more easily intelligible.

---

* Vide Justificative Appendix to Chapter VI.

120   CHAPTER VI.

Way taken by the Socinian system.	Way taken by the Evangelical system.	Way taken by the Orthodox Church of England system.	Way taken by the Apostolical system.	Way taken by the Roman-Catholic system.
No. 1.	No. 2.	No. 3.	No. 4.	No. 5.

Now upon a review of the case under consideration, as it stands established above, and is palpably presented to us (if we may so speak) in the annexed synopsis, we perceive, we intuitively comprehend, the character and degree of that error into which the Authors of the system of the Oxford Tracts have fallen, when they attempt to frame a religious system, constituted upon the principle of holding the *via media* between the Reformers and the Romanists.

It is scarcely necessary to intimate, that by taking (as they do) the Protestantism spoken of, or (as is the same thing) the religious system of the Reformers, to be the extreme or cardinal error that stands opposed to Popery, which it is not; and also assuming that the religious system which they have framed, upon the principle adverted to, is identical with the orthodox system of the Church of England, when, in point of fact, it differs from it (as we have seen) essentially and irreconcileably;—the Authors of the system of the Oxford Tracts err in precisely the same manner, and to exactly the same degree, as they would do if they falsified the specification of particulars stated in the annexed synopsis, and surreptitiously assigned a central position to the compartment which we have designated as No. 4, by substituting No. 2 for No. 1, and classing Nos. 3 and 4 together, or merging, rather, the former in the latter.

We would observe, in conclusion, that from the

state of the case as it stands established above, a most important general conclusion is deducible.

It is a principle which the universal consent of mankind has stamped with the character of " a certainty of reason," that 'truth' is ever to be found in a mean between two opposite, and, if we may so speak, anti-correspondent errors. True courage, for instance, is found in, and may be said to occupy, the mean between the two opposite and anti-correspondent errors (or false qualities, we should rather term them, in this case) of rashness and cowardice.*

And this being the case; and since (as we have seen) the orthodox system of the Church of England holds the *via media*, or preserves a mean, as nearly as possible, between the two extreme opposite and anti-correspondent errors of Popery and Socinianism, and between the two mean opposite and anti-correspondent errors of the Evangelical and Apostolical systems; it must be entitled, it is evident, to that character of truth with which the principle adverted to is capable of investing it: it follows, therefore, that we may safely conclude, that the orthodox system of the Church of England is a true, or (in other words) the right, system.†

---

* Vide Appendix, No. 2. † Vide Appendix, No. 3.

JUSTIFICATIVE APPENDIX TO CHAP. VI.

In the preface to the " Letters to the Authors of the Plain Tracts for Times," it is stated that, " It is simply because it is the most convenient, from being the most generally recognise d, appellation of the party of which he has occasion to speak, and of the doctrines they profess; and not in the invidious sense which was formerly attached to it; that the Author has adopted and employs the term ' Evangelical.' " And the term, it is scarcely necessary to observe, is used in the same sense when it is employed above.

It is, of course, allowable to term the system of the Authors of the Oxford Tracts the ' Apostolical system;' as they themselves have designated it thus.

It will, no doubt, be considered to be incumbent upon us to adduce some definite proof that the orthodox system of the Church of England takes the *via media* between the Evangelical and Apostolical systems.

In proceeding to do so, we would observe, that, according to the system of the Evangelical party in our Church, baptism is ' a mere initiatory rite, which constitutes the appointed means of admission into the visible Church;' it is ' a rite ' (we add lest our former definition should be supposed to be inaccurate), which is not attended by any divine efficacy by which either regeneration or justification is wrought.'

According to the system of the Authors of the Oxford Tracts, baptism is a sacrament by which justification is immediately effected.

Now when the orthodox system of the Church of England teaches (as it does) that baptism ' is a sacrament by which regeneration is wrought;' or is ' a rite ' (in other words) ' which, by virtue of a divine efficacy with which the Almighty has been pleased to invest it, has the effect of implanting certain godly susceptibilities in the soul, which are, as it were, the seed of that true and lively faith which constitutes the *origo originata* of justification (according to the orthodox system of the Church of England); and which, when so implanted, may either fructify, as it were, and, in consequence, produce the plant of faith and fruit of justification; or rot, if we may so speak, and perish in barrenness:' it evidently preserves the mean as nearly as possible—a mean as exact as any which it is possible for us to indicate—between a system which regards baptism as 'an initiatory rite which has no sort of influence upon, or connexion with, justification,' and a system which regards baptism as 'an ordinance which is the direct and immediate instrument of effecting justification.'

We might easily have adduced other equally convincing proof of the truth of our assertion that the orthodox system of the Church of England holds the *via media* between the mean errors of the Evangelical and Apostolical systems; but it is, obviously, needless to do so, after we have established it so incontrovertibly in the important instance adverted to above.

No. 2.

It was (we have little doubt) from a recognition of, and confidence in, the truth of the principle adverted to above, that the Authors of the system of the Oxford Tracts were led to make their attempt to establish a religious system constituted upon the principle of holding the *via media* between the Reformers and the Romanists.

No. 3.

As true courage, be it observed, is found in the mean, or holds the *via media*, we may say (for the forms of expression are synonymous) between the two extreme opposite and anti-correspondent errors or false qualities of rashness and cowardice; so, it also occupies the mean, or holds the *via media* between the two mean opposite and anti-correspondent errors or false qualities of temerity and timidity.

It is evident, therefore, that the case stated above, is analogous in every particular to that which we have established, when we shewed, in the course of the preceding pages, that the orthodox system of the Church of England holds the *via media* between the two extreme opposite or anti-correspondent errors or erroneous courses taken by Popery and Socinianism and the two mean opposite or anti-correspondent errors or erroneous courses taken by the evangelical and apostolical systems.

And the analogy, be it observed! which subsists between the two cases, is not of a mere formal or external description only, but one of an intimate (if we may so speak) and intrinsic character.

For 'cowardice of belief' and fear of believing—it would be to ascribe wilfulness to the Socinian, were to say 'a determination not to believe'—any thing above, or incomprehensible, by human reason, may truly and very intelligibly be said to lie at the root, and constitute, as it were, the radical principle of the errors of the Socinian system: and so, a 'rashness of belief'—a hardihood of credulity truly marvellous, under the influence of which men hesitate not to receive a dogma, of which the impossibility is self-evident to reason and the falsehood palpable to sense; may as truly and as intelligibly be said to lie at the root of, and constitute, as it were, the radical principle of the errors of the Romish system: whilst it is a principle allied to, or diverging towards, but not actually degenerating into, 'cowardice of belief,' that withholds the Evangelical churchman from assenting to the doctrine of baptismal regeneration, or recognising the apostolic succession, and is otherwise operative in generating the errors discoverable in the Evangelical system; and it is a principle allied to, or diverging towards, but not (as for the sake of argument we assume) actually degenerating into 'a rashness of belief,' which has led, as it appears, to the adoption of the errors peculiar to the apostolical system.

We have not, be it observed! thus minutely traced the analogy observable between the two cases adverted to, merely with a view of displaying our ingenuity (as an inattentive reader may, possibly, be apt to surmise): but because, inasmuch as it is universally admitted to be a self-evident truth ' that true courage occupies the mean, or takes the *via media* between cowardice and rashness, and also between temerity and timidity;' it follows, that by shewing that an analogy so close and intimate as that which we have pointed out, subsists between a case or

CHAPTER VI.

position which is admitted to contain a self-evident truth, and the case or position which we have established with respect to the orthodox system of the Church of England; we effect that which must, of necessity, produce a distinct and irresistible conviction in favour of the latter, upon every mind of an unaffected ingenuousness.

ADDITIONAL APPENDIX.

For fear lest any transgressor might otherwise wrest what has been said, with respect to the case of the Earl of Rochester, to his own prejudice, we deem it incumbent upon us to subjoin certain reflections made by Bishop Burnet upon the subject. Before we do so, however, we must beg to premise, that it is manifestly impossible, that the fact, that such may be the case, can afford the shadow of an objection to the doctrine holden by the orthodox system of our Church, with respect to the *origo originata* of justification; inasmuch as we know, that men of perverse minds may wrest the Holy Scriptures themselves to their destruction.

"Men should not," Bishop Burnet says, " take the least encouragement to themselves in that desperate and unreasonable resolution of puttiug off their repentance till they can sin no longer, from the hopes I have expressed of this Lord's obtaining mercy at the last, and from thence presume, that they also shall be received when they turn to God on their death-beds: for what mercy soever God may shew to such as really never were inwardly touched before that time, yet there is no reason to think, that those who have dealt so disingenuously with God and their own souls, as designedly to put off their turning to him upon such considerations, would then be accepted of Him."

BY THE SAME AUTHOR.

Published by T. Cadell, Strand,

LETTERS to the AUTHORS of the PLAIN TRACTS for CRITICAL TIMES.
Price 6s. cloth lettered.

ALSO,

A Reprint of Dr. HORNECK'S TREATISE on the LORD'S SUPPER, entitled The CRUCIFIED JESUS:
With
A LIFE OF THE AUTHOR.
Price 6s. 6d.

www.ingramcontent.com/pod-product-compliance
Lightning Source LLC
LaVergne TN
LVHW081353060426
835510LV00013B/1806